Embracing
GOD'S WORLD

Published by
The Bible Reading Fellowship
15 The Chambers, Vineyard
Abingdon OX14 3FE
Website: www.brf.org.uk

ISBN 978 1 84101 574 3

First published 1996 by Hodder & Stoughton Ltd
This edition published 2007
10 9 8 7 6 5 4 3 2 1 0
All rights reserved

Acknowledgments
Unless otherwise stated, scripture quotations are taken from the *Holy Bible, New International Version*, copyright © 1973, 1978, 1984 by International Bible Society. Used by permission of Hodder & Stoughton Publishers, a division of Hodder Headline Ltd. All rights reserved. 'NIV' is a registered trademark of International Bible Society. UK trademark number 1448790.

Scripture quotations taken from THE MESSAGE, copyright © by Eugene H. Peterson 1993, 1994, 1995. Used by permission of NavPress Publishing Group.

Scriptures quoted from the Good News Bible published by The Bible Societies/HarperCollins Publishers Ltd, UK © American Bible Society 1966, 1971, 1976, 1992, used with permission.

Extracts from *I Am With You* by John Woolley reproduced by kind permission of O Books, www.O-books.net

Prayer reprinted from *Love: A Guide for Prayer*, by Jacqueline Syrup Bergan and S. Marie Schwan, copyright 1984, 2004. Published by The Word Among Us Press, Ijamsville, Maryland, U.S., www.wordamongus.org. Used with permission.

Prayer by George Appleton reprinted from *The Oxford Book of Prayer*, ed. George Appleton, OUP, 2002. Used by permission of Oxford University Press.

Prayer by Eddie Askew reprinted from *A Silence and a Shouting*, The Leprosy Mission International, 1982. Used with permission.

Every effort has been made to trace copyright holders for other extracts included in this book. We apologize for any omissions and invite copyright holders to contact the publisher so that we may include their details in any future reprint.

A catalogue record for this book is available from the British Library.

Printed in Singapore by Craft Print International Ltd

Embracing
GOD'S WORLD
Prayers for the yearning heart

JOYCE HUGGETT

*For the Sisters of Bethany, with profound thanks
for your prayers and for providing me with a
special place 'to be'*

Acknowledgments

When I agreed to collate this book of prayers, I never imagined that the project would bring so many new friends into my life. Corresponding with the authors of some of the prayers I have quoted was a humbling and enriching experience as well as one that widened considerably my circle of friends.

To write a prayer is to reveal an intimate part of oneself—that hidden part we normally expose to God but to few other people. To have a prayer published is to share with countless strangers as well as friends some of one's spiritual secrets. Yet, when I invited former strangers as well as familiar friends to contribute to the compilation of prayers and poems that make up this book, they were more than generous with their response. For this and for the richness and warmth of the correspondence that was generated prior to publication, I shall always be grateful.

As always, I also owe a debt of gratitude to the countless people who prayed this book into being. Supported by their interest and prayer, inspiration flowed and energized me—even when I was battling with a debilitating virus.

My husband, David, and James Catford, who edited the first edition of the book, also provided me with endless encouragement. I drew strength from their interest, support and prayer, for which I shall always be grateful. My friend Pauline Gallagher provided me with a great deal of practical help when I had reached the proofreading stage of this publication. I look back on her support with gratitude and affection.

I found myself tremendously moved while typing some of the prayers and poems that lie between this book's covers. Behind each 'piece' lies a wealth of experience, sometimes of untold suffering and always of self-dedication. For these reasons, I count it a great privilege to spread before readers the expressions of commitment of so many of God's unsung heroes and heroines.

More recently, Naomi Starkey has added to the encouragement mentioned above. Since she was the one to suggest that this book should go into print once more, I trust that it will prove to be a blessing to many of its readers—including those to whom I have dedicated this new edition. They have given so much to me that it will be heart-warming to think of them being enriched by the prayers that appear on these pages.

CONTENTS

INTRODUCTION

Compassionate caring is the acid test of the authentic Christ-following life... the Christlike person formed gradually by the Spirit will be characterised by an ever-growing responsiveness and sensitivity to the pain of others... Compassion, in the way of Jesus, places our lives beside those in turmoil, seeks understanding of their anguish and labours with them for the sake of their greater wholeness.[1]

Over the years, those far-reaching claims have been woven into the very fibre of my being. The process began in a life-changing way shortly after the publication of my book *Listening to God*. That book describes how I found myself being drawn into experiences of prayer that I had not previously explored—namely, contemplative prayer and charismatic prayer. To mark the publication of the book, my local radio station, BBC Radio Nottingham, broadcast an interview with me during which Jeremy, the interviewer, invited me to tell listeners a little more of my story. Jeremy was obviously intrigued so, when the interview was over, as we sat chatting over a cup of coffee, he asked his most dynamic question of the morning: 'Joyce! I'm interested that there's no reference to social justice in *Listening to God*. Yet surely, prayer and social justice go together? Maybe that will be the subject of your next book?'

The subject of my next book was not social justice, though it was about compassion for others. Several years were to elapse before I was to write with conviction: 'The closer we come to the compassionate Christ, the more we will catch his compassion for his world—particularly the world of the poor and the marginalized.' Several more years passed before I heard and responded to God's call to leave the comparative comfort of my familiar small corner of the world and consent to being catapulted into the great unknown of living and working among Christian overseas workers.

One of the ways in which God jolted me out of my complacency into an awareness that he wanted to send me to far-flung corners of the world was through a meditation popularized by St Ignatius of Loyola. In this meditation, we are invited to step back in time to the pre-Christian era—those days before the birth of Christ when the voice of God seemed strangely silent. We are invited, too, to imagine ourselves sitting in the heavenly places with the Holy Trinity: Father, Son and Holy Spirit. As the three members of the Holy Trinity look down on a world hurtling to destruction, we gaze at the world also. As I recorded in my journal after I had embarked on this meditation:

I found it awesome to sit with the Father, the Son and the Holy Spirit to take a peep at today's world. Tanzania, where I once encountered children begging for pencils so that they could attend school. Kenya, where the standard of living is comparatively high and yet pathetically low compared to the lifestyle we take for granted in the West. Poland, where Christians still struggle to survive. Eastern Europe, where thousands are turning to Christ but where most people live below the poverty line. The town where I live, where good, generous people live alongside drunkards, those who overeat, those who exploit girls from the east as well as the west, those who are greedy for gain.

As now, so then. The Father, the Son and the Holy Spirit watched the world hurtle to disaster, and the Holy Trinity did not remain unmoved. The moment had clearly come to put 'Operation Rescue' into motion. So the angel Gabriel was sent to the little town of Nazareth to inform Mary that she was to become the mother of the Messiah. Mary, a woman dear to God's heart, 'blessed among women', not because she could boast rank or reputation but because she was as soft clay in the Creator's hands. Mary, whose heart had already been turned to her Saviour and who, by her ready 'yes' and by God's grace, made possible the impossible. Mary, who, now pregnant with Christ, carried the Saviour of the world wherever she went—to family and friends, to the village well or the bazaar on the hillside.

As I pondered these mysteries, God seemed to read my struggles and speak into them. I wanted to be like Mary, ready to say 'yes' to whatever God would ask of me. The week before, I had rededicated my life to God and his service. But to be like Mary! Was such readiness possible? My mind focused only on those treasures I might be asked to renounce: family, friends, the familiarity of home, country and culture.

'Nothing is impossible with me,' God implored. 'You don't have to renounce anything, but rather receive Someone. The Holy Spirit will fill you just as he overshadowed Mary. Remember that Mary was not asked to renounce anything but rather to receive an incredible gift—the privilege of becoming the mother of the Messiah.'

'Mary was not asked to renounce anything but to receive an incredible gift. God longs to impregnate us with his divine energy and power,' I wrote in my journal. I was on a five-week retreat at the time. By the end of that retreat, I had indeed been overshadowed afresh by God's life-changing Spirit. He had injected into me a passion for the world that was new to me, even though it was but a pale reflection of the Holy Trinity's passion for the universe and its people.

From that moment onwards, embracing God's world became a passion. That is why, when I first collated the prayers that appear in this book, I chose *Embracing God's World* as the title. The title was inspired by a small booklet entitled *Embrace the World* that I had stumbled on while I was on another retreat in Singapore. The booklet contains sayings penned by a woman of God whose passion for the world prompted her to write prayers like this:

O Jesus,
You are my life,
my Beloved,
my all.
I offer you my life,
I give you my heart,
I wish what you wish,
nothing but your holy will.[2]

The booklet also breathed out exhortations and reflections like these: 'Courage! How many persons will owe their lives to your sacrifices?'[3] 'Remember, all your strength comes from God.'[4] 'O! How beautiful is the prayer of a person who in silence listens to God's voice.'[5] 'Only in solitude and silence can God's voice be heard in our hearts.'[6]

For many years, I used that booklet daily. When I was weary, the exhortations encouraged me in the sense that they poured courage into me. When I found myself drawn into the still, focused place of prayer, the reflections brought a sense of harmony and peace— God's *shalom*.

The booklet reminds me of one of the places where I used to pray on the retreat in Singapore. In the cottage where I stayed, one of the rooms had been converted into a chapel. I would kneel or lie prostrate on the floor of that chapel and gaze at the map of the world that covered the wall opposite me. A picture of Mary adoring the Christ-child nestled in the corner of the map while, over Cyprus, where I lived at that time, hung an illuminated circle on which was inscribed God's promise: 'I shall put my Spirit in you.' The picture and the promise reminded me of some of the ways God had persuaded me to embrace his world.

'Do share some of your own prayers,' the editor of the first edition of this book insisted when I agreed to collate the prayers that fill the pages of *Embracing God's World*. At first I resisted this request. For me, prayer is intensely personal. Much of it is conducted in silence; most of it is wordless, so I feared there would be little to quote. When I do write prayers, I write them for God, not for publication. It never occurred to me that anyone would want to publish them. My prayers that appear in this book, therefore— prayers that can be identified by the initials LJH—are not polished poetry or prose but words that my pen has whispered to God. Some were written on the retreats I have mentioned, others during equally life-changing moments of my prayer pilgrimage. I share them for one reason only—because there are times in my life when I am stuck for words to pray or when the stream of my own spontaneous wordless prayer dries up or when I simply sense the rightness of approaching God through words offered by others under the inspiration of the Holy Spirit. Time and time again, I have found that those who have penned their prayers, whether they lived thousands of years ago or whether they are my contemporaries, have breathed the prayer that my heart yearns to echo. With relief, therefore, I pray them, personalizing them in such a way that I can make of them an offering to God. I quote some of these prayers alongside my own in *Embracing God's World*. If any of my prayers are ever treasured by my readers in the way I treasure some of the prayers I have quoted here, I shall be both humbled and joyful.

Enjoying intimacy with God

The desire to sacrifice for Christ, for some people, is born in the place of intimacy with God. I sense that we see this happening in the life of Mary of Bethany (see Luke 10:38–42). When her gregarious sister, Martha, invited Jesus into their home, Mary found herself drawn by Jesus' magnetism to nestle at his feet. There, doubtless, she found herself on the receiving end of his love for, wherever Jesus went, love flowed from him. John makes it clear in his Gospel that Mary reciprocated the Master's love. One way she expressed her adoration was to anoint Jesus with her most precious possession: the perfume she was probably saving for her wedding day (John 12:3).

Did Jesus share with her, in those moments of delicious intimacy, the reason why he was visiting Bethany at that moment in time? Did he tell her what he had been attempting for months to impress on his disciples: that he was on his way to Jerusalem, where he would be butchered to death? It seems probable that he did divulge these secrets. Is that not the reason why, in John 12, we find Mary sidling alongside Jesus at the supper party? Is that not the reason why she prepared him for his burial with that memorable sacrifice that filled the air with its fragrance?

According to Jesus, Mary had discovered 'the one essential thing' (Luke 10:42)—the value of soaking up, absorbing, person-alizing the elixir of the divine love. It was as she drank these draughts of love and later feasted on them by pondering them that her heart was stirred and she conceived the desire to express her devotion in self-sacrificing service—even taking the risk of doing so in public.

As for Mary, so for us. When we create time to assimilate the fact that we are God's cherished children, little by little our hearts lose their hardness. In the soft centre of our being, the desire to sacrifice self for the Beloved is born. One reason for this is that, where true love exists, it yearns to please and promote the well-being of the loved one. Another reason is that, when we both grasp and digest the love of another, we hear that healing, liberating message: we are accepted, valued, wanted. This message nourishes, nurtures and affirms us in such a way that it generates within us the desire to achieve great things for the loved one—albeit in a hidden, humble way. That is why the first section of this book consists of murmurings written by those who have lingered in the presence of God, relished intimacy with him and yearned for an even deeper relationship with him. Such intimacy can, of course, be sought as an escape from the harsh realities of life, but if the intimacy being enjoyed is truly with Christ, the Saviour of the world, his compassion for a weary world will, in time, rub off on us. His compassion is contagious. The closer we come to him, the closer we shall identify with his heart's longing to rescue the world and those that live in it.

Some of the prayers are simple, ordinary, even domestic. Others are more majestic, even grand. Each of them begs the would-be pray-er to read them as slowly as possible—to savour them and, where appropriate, to echo them or to allow them to trigger a prayer of their own.

LIKE MARY

A woman in the crowd called out, 'Blessed is the mother who gave you birth and nursed you.' Jesus replied: 'Blessed rather are those who hear the word of God and obey it.'

LUKE 11:27–28

I am the Lord, your Saviour…
I want you to enter into my love.
Yes, I want you to come so close to me that
I can speak my love into your heart.

I want to come to you as I came to Mary.
I look on you as I looked on Mary.

I am not looking at your greatness
nor at your attempts at asserting yourself
or trying to stand out from others.
I see your littleness.
I see deep within you—
behind all your various disguises,
masks and roles—
I see the child,
my beloved child who is hungry and cries
for my love.
Come to me.
Rest in me.
Stay with me…

I am the Lord, your Saviour.
I want to come to you now and enfold you with my love
on all sides.

I do not want to drill my love into your life.
I want to bring it to birth in you.

Mary's task is yours too.
To receive Jesus into your life and to bring
my love to birth into your world.
In that way I can use you as a channel
for my love.

Through you I can love the people I send
in your path.
I can use your eyes to look at them
with my goodness.
I can use your ears to listen to them.
I can use your mouth to speak to them.

Rest now in my Love.
Then I can do great things for you too.
And through you.

TRANS. SR LISBETH CHN

LOVE

Lord my God, when your love spilled over
      into creation
            you thought of me.
               I am
from love,   of love,   for love.
      Let my heart, O God, always
          recognise,
              cherish,
             and enjoy your goodness in all of creation.
      Direct all that is me toward your praise.
Teach me reverence for every person, all things,
      energise me in your service.
               Lord God,
      may nothing ever distract me from your love…

neither health nor sickness,
wealth nor poverty,
honour nor dishonour,
long life nor short life.
May I never seek nor choose to be other
than you intend or wish.

JACQUELINE SYRUP BERGAN AND SR MARIE SCHWAN [1]

MY LORD, MY LIFE

Mary sat at the feet of Jesus and listened. She soaked up Jesus' love and responded with reciprocal love. Love prompted her to act—to donate to Jesus her most precious possession. We, too, may sit at the feet of Christ and absorb his love. Unlike Mary, we cannot anoint the feet of the Beloved. We can, however, touch and minister to the needs of the poor instead, knowing that whatever we do for the least of Christ's brothers or sisters, we do for him.

You yourself are my contemplation;
You are my delight.
You for your own sake
I seek above me;
from you yourself I feed within me.
You are the field in which I labour;
You are the fruit for which I labour.
You are my cause;
You are my effect.
You are my beginning;
You are my end without end.
You are for me eternity.

LJH [2]

ALL IN ALL

True knowledge of me comes when I am valued... To place me above everything else in your life is indispensable to your growth... causing you to thrill at the thought of me, and to desire closer and closer communion with me.

When you arrive at the blessed state of my being all in all to you, you also realise that this has not made any less precious those whom you love on earth... On the contrary, my place of supremacy in your life encircles those other ties, and means that the influence of heaven is in your relationships—making them pleasing to me.

JOHN WOOLLEY [3]

Come, my Light, and illumine my darkness.
Come, my Life, and revive me from death.
Come, my Physician, and heal my wounds.
Come, Flame of divine love,
and burn up the thorns of my sins, kindling my heart with the flame of thy love.
Come, my King, sit upon the throne of my heart and reign there.
For thou alone art my King and my Lord.

ST DIMITRI OF ROSTOV (1651–1709)

You shone upon me with brilliant radiance and, so it seemed, you appeared to me in your wholeness as with my whole self I gazed openly upon you. And when I said, 'Master, who are you?' then you were pleased to speak for the first time with me the prodigal. With what gentleness did you talk to me, as I stood astonished and trembling, as I reflected a little within myself and said: 'What does this glory and this dazzling brightness mean? How is it that I am chosen to receive such great blessings?'

'I am God,' you replied, 'who became man for your sake; and because you have sought me with your whole heart, see from this time onwards you shall be my brother, my fellow-heir, and my friend.'

ST SYMEON THE NEW THEOLOGIAN (949–1022)

O gracious and holy Father,
give us wisdom to perceive you,
intelligence to understand you,
diligence to seek you,
eyes to behold you,
a life to proclaim you,
and a heart to meditate on you,
through the power of the Spirit of Jesus Christ our Lord.
ST BENEDICT (c.480–543)

O Lord our God,
whose might is invincible,
whose glory is incomprehensible,
whose mercy is immeasurable
and whose love towards mankind is unspeakable…
look down upon us…
and show us your abundant mercy and compassion.
LJH [4]

Lord Jesus our Saviour,
    let us now come to you;
Our hearts are cold;
    Lord, warm them by your selfless love;
Our hearts are sinful;
    cleanse them with your precious blood.
Our hearts are weak;
    strengthen them with your joyous Spirit.
Our hearts are empty;
    fill them with your divine presence.

Lord Jesus, our hearts are yours;
    possess them always
    and only for
    yourself.
ST AUGUSTINE OF HIPPO (354–430)

I know that the Immovable comes down;
I know that the Invisible appears to me;
I know that he who is far outside the whole creation
Takes me within himself and hides me in his arms…
I, a frail, small mortal in the world,
Behold the Creator of the world, all of him, within myself;
And I know that I shall not die, for I am within the Life,
I have the whole of Life springing up as a fountain within me.
You are within my heart, you are in heaven:
Both there and here you show yourself to me with equal glory.
LJH [5]

MOTHER GOD

I have stilled and quietened my soul;
like a weaned child with its mother,
like a weaned child is my soul within me.
PSALM 131:2

Lord,
hold me as a mother holds her baby
because you love me.
Not because I'm hurt or sick,
but just because you love me.
Caress my forehead.
Gaze tenderly into my eyes.
Kiss me.
Rock me gently and sing me a love song.
Teach me, Lord, to love you as a child loves its mother,
to rest in you as a baby rests in its mother's arms,
    its mother's lap—
content and completely fulfilled.
SCW

And you, Jesus, are you not also a mother?
Are you not the mother, who, like a hen,
gathers her chickens under her wings...

And you, my soul, dead in yourself,
run under the wings of Jesus your mother
and lament your griefs under his feathers.
Ask that your wounds may be healed
and that, comforted, you may live again.

Christ, my mother,
you gather your chickens under your wings;
this dead chicken of yours puts himself under those wings.
For by your gentleness the badly frightened are comforted,
by your sweet smell the despairing are revived,
your warmth gives life to the dead,
your touch justifies sinners.
Mother, know again your dead child,
both by the sign of the cross and the voice of confession.
Warm your chicken...
justify your sinner.
Let your terrified one be consoled by you;
despairing of himself, let him be comforted by you;
and in your whole and unceasing grace
let him be refashioned by you.
For from you flows consolation for sinners;
to you be blessing for ages and ages. Amen.

ST ANSELM (1033–1109), ABBREVIATED

HOLD ME CLOSE

If you are consciously relaxing in my love, others can truly receive me through yourself. You are then a source of joy, reassurance and peace to them.

JOHN WOOLLEY [6]

Often, we're not able to reach out to others because we are hurting too much ourselves. When we know that God cherishes us in the way this prayer describes, the nature of our service may well change. We no longer serve out of duty or for the fun of fulfilment. We serve from desire.

Hold me close, Lord;
I so easily feel alone-ness.
May I be aware of your ever-present reality in my life.

My child—
I chose you;
I planned for you;
I brought you into being.
I gave you to your family;
I entrusted you to them;
though my heart ached
to know that I could not protect you
from all the knocks and hurts that would come.

I've walked beside you all the way;
I've walked behind and gone before,
and walked by your side.
Nothing has come to you that I didn't know about.
Though the enemy would have mauled you
as a lion mauls a lamb
or a bear cub,
I never let him.

Trust me, trust me,
know that I love you,
know that I care deeply for one who is mine,
mine,
MINE.

SCW

AVAILABLE FOR YOU

Lord,
I offer what I am
to what you are.
I stretch up to you in desire
my attention on you alone.
I cannot grasp you,
   explain you,
   describe you,
only cast myself into the depths
   of your mystery,
only let your love pierce the
   cloud of my unknowing.
Let me forget all but you.
You are what I long for.
You are my chiefest good.
You are my eager hope.
You are my allness.

In the glimpses of your eternity.
   your unconditional freedom,
   your unfailing wisdom,
   your perfect love,
I am humble and worshipping,
   warming to love and hope,
   waiting and available
   for your will,
   dear Lord.

GEORGE APPLETON (1902–93)[7]

FOLLOWING JESUS

Dear Lord and Father of mankind,
forgive our foolish ways!
Re-clothe us in our rightful mind,
in purer lives thy service find,
in deeper reverence praise.

In simple trust like theirs who heard,
beside the Syrian sea,
the gracious calling of the Lord,
let us, like them, without a word,
rise up and follow thee.

Drop thy still dews of quietness,
till all our strivings cease:
take from our souls the strain and stress,
and let our ordered lives confess
the beauty of thy peace.

JOHN GREENLEAF WHITTIER (1807–92)

HUNGRY AND THIRSTY FOR GOD'S PRESENCE

Dear Lord,
teach me to pray.
For just as the deer pants for cool water
so my heart hungers for you.
My soul is parched and dry;
I thirst for your presence, my living Lord.
I will carve out a place for you.
Lord, hear my prayer
in that place,
in every place—
come to me and meet me.

LJH

Jesus, Thou joy of loving hearts!
Thou fount of life, thou light of men!
From the best bliss that earth imparts
we turn unfilled to thee again.

BERNARD OF CLAIRVAUX (1090–1153), TRANS. RAY PALMER, 1858

YOUR SERVANT IS LISTENING

Speak, Lord, for your servant is listening.
    O, Lord, my heart is ready,
    my mind awake, attentive, alert;
    my spirit open and ardent,
    abandoning all else,
    holding itself in leash,
    straining the eye of faith,
    hearkening for your step, distant and nearer,
    leaping with love,
    throbbing loudly, yet lying still.

Speak, Lord, for your servant is listening.

LJH[8]

MY LIFE, MY ALL

O Jesus,
you are my life,
my beloved,
my all.
I offer my life,
I give you my heart,
I wish what you wish,
nothing but your holy will.

ST MARY EUPHRASIA[9]

AT PEACE

You are my peace, O Lord.
From the thousand wearinesses of the day-to-day,
from the disappointments,
from the nervous and senseless haste,
I turn to you
and am at peace.
The clamour dies.
I spring to life in the sunshine of your presence.
Even so, come, Lord Jesus
to this heart of mine.

LJH

THE FOCUS OF GOD'S LOVE

Father,
In this place of prayer
I feel your everlasting arms
enfolding me
caressing me
cradling me
in the embrace of never-ending love.
For your tenderness
I praise you;
that I am the focus of your love
I thank you
and surrender myself to you,
though all too feeble
is my response of love to Love.

LJH

YOU CAME

All day long on my bed
I looked for the one my heart loves;
I looked for him but did not find him.
I will get up now and… search for the one my heart loves.
So I looked for him but did not find him.
The watchmen found me
as they made their rounds in the city.
'Have you seen the one my heart loves?'
Scarcely had I passed them
when I found the one my heart loves.
I held him and would not let him go
till I had brought him to my mother's house,
to the room of the one who conceived me.

SONG OF SONGS 3:1–4, ADAPTED

I had just written that when he came:

Silently, surreptitiously,
he overwhelmed me,
ravished me,
held me.
He loved me,
filled me,
and he left me.
But I am no longer bereft,
just dazed.
Enraptured.
Re-captivated.
Conquered.
Lost in wonder,
    love
    and praise.

No words,
   no music,
      no drawing
can express this inexpressible joy.
Only wonder.
   Only love.
      Only praise.
         Only the sounds of silent adoration.

LJH

SUSTENANCE AND SUSTAINER

Beloved—
I need you.
Without you I cannot exist.
You are my sustenance
and my Sustainer.
Turn me from all lesser loves
To Love.
Succour and strengthen me
Tonight and always.
Amen

LJH

TEACH ME TO LISTEN

Teach me to listen, Holy Spirit,
for your voice—
in busyness and in boredom,
in certainty and in doubt,
in noise and in silence.

AUTHOR UNKNOWN [10]

ENJOYING INTIMACY AT ALL TIMES

Lord of my heart, give me vision to inspire me,
that working or resting, I may always think of you.
Lord of my heart, give me light to guide me,
that at home or abroad, I may always walk in your way.
Lord of my heart, give me wisdom to direct me,
that thinking or acting, I may always discern right from wrong.
Lord of my heart, give me courage to strengthen me,
that amongst friends or enemies, I may always proclaim your
justice.
Lord of my heart, give me trust to console me,
that hungry or well-fed, I may always rely on your mercy.
Heart of my own heart, whatever may befall me,
rule over my thoughts and feelings, my words and actions. Amen

AUTHOR UNKNOWN

REMEMBERING

This prayer was written when I was recalling God's goodness to us
in the aftermath of a car crash in the former Yugoslavia. Our Dor-
mobile was a write-off so we were forced to travel home by train.
While we were jouneying through Italy, an unknown passenger
came up to my husband and pressed into his hand some £20
worth of lire so that we could buy food for the journey. Earlier in
the trip, Yugoslav peasants had shared their picnic with us.

For every memory of your faithfulness,
my Father,
I give you thanks and praise.
When we were destitute,
you proved yourself to be an abundant God.
Aware, afresh,
of the length and breadth,

29

the height and depth
of your love,
I pray that, even now,
my roots may be burrowing ever deeper
into the love that will not let me go
so that, when changes shake those roots,
my trust in you may remain strong and firm.
LJH

SOLITUDE

Solitude at last.
Beauty
Tranquillity
Familiarity
Shalom
Soft songs sung by birds.

In this place where your peace permeates my pain,
and where I feel the gravitational pull of love, Lord,
I begin to feel
not fragmented,
but focused,
in harmony with you,
with your creation,
with my situation.
I begin to gain a new perspective—
your perspective.
I begin to enter into your rest.
For this, I give you heartfelt thanks
and praise.
LJH

GOD'S LOVE

Father,
I pray that out of the wealth of your glory
you will strengthen my inner being with your Spirit,
so that Christ will make his home in my heart,
and so that I may have my roots in love
and make love the foundation
of my entire existence.
I pray that you will reveal to me
just how broad and long,
how high and deep
the love of Christ is,
so that I may be filled to overflowing
with the very nature of Christ.
IJH[11]

Lord, your love is a persevering love
that brings me back,
that renews a sense of perspective,
that woos and wins me again and again.
For this undeserved, unearned gift
I feel eternally grateful.
IJH

THE PEARL OF GREAT PRICE

You, O Lord, are the one that I long for
And yet
I'm not sure that I can bear the emptiness
that this longing will involve.
If I really long for you
then there will be no room
for the clutter of a lot of other longings.

I must be hollowed out
to become a capacity for you.
I shrink from the pain that that will involve.
But I must needs feel the poverty of my emptiness
and my poverty meets with your giving
in the silence of lovers.

I feel this emptiness as an ache,
a frustration,
as I realize that what I want, dear Lord,
more than anything else in the world
is that my life should revolve around *you*,
the pearl of great price;
that I should be able to take others deeper into you,
that I might be able to take your love into the hearts of others.
Give me the grace to go on and on
wanting you more than anything or anyone.

FIRST TWO VERSES: AUTHOR UNKNOWN; THIRD VERSE: LJH

A PRAYER OF AUGUSTINE OF HIPPO

Late have I loved you, O beauty ever ancient, ever new!
Late have I loved you
and behold, you were within, and I without,
    and without I sought you.
And deformed, I ran after those forms of beauty
    you have made.
You were with me, and I was not with you,
those things held me back from you,
things whose only being was to be in you.
You called;
you cried,
and broke in through my deafness.

You flashed;
you shone,
and you chased away my blindness.
You became fragrant,
and I inhaled and sighed for you.
I tasted,
and now hunger and thirst for you.
You touched me,
and I burned for your embrace.

DAY BY DAY

O gentle flame of the life of Christ,
enfold and fill my heart afresh
as each new day is born.

SISTER THERESA MARGARET CHN

PSALM 139

O God, you know me inside out,
   through and through.

Everything I do,
   every thought that flits through my mind,
   every step I take,
   every plan I make,
   every word I speak
you know, even before these things happen.

You know my past.
You know my future.

Your circumventing presence covers my every move.
Your knowledge of me sometimes comforts me,
    sometimes frightens me,
    but always it is far beyond my comprehension.

There is no way to escape you, no place to hide.
If I ascend to the heights of joy
    you are there before me.
If I am plunged into the depths of despair
    you are there to meet me.
I could fly to the other side of the world
    and find you there to lead the way.
I could walk into the darkest of nights
    only to find you there
    to lighten its dismal hours.

You were present at my very conception.
You guided the moulding of my unformed members
    within the body of my mother.
Nothing about me, from beginning to end,
    was hid from your eyes.
How wonderful it all is.

May your all-knowing, everywhere-present Spirit
    continue to search out my feelings and thoughts.
Deliver me from all that may hurt or destroy me
    and guide me along the paths of love and truth.

AUTHOR UNKNOWN

Help me to say 'Yes'

In his powerful and moving book, *The Life of the Beloved*, Henri Nouwen reminds us that we are intimately loved long before our parents or teachers, our spouse, our children or friends loved or wounded us. This insight, he claims, is a truth that deserves to be claimed by each person on earth. It is a truth declared by the one who underlines it when he says those priceless words: 'You are my beloved.'

When we really listen to that voice with inner attentiveness, Nouwen reminds us, we will hear at the very centre of our being words that insist that we are intimately and uniquely loved by God. Every time we hear and heed such a reminder, we will discover within ourselves a longing, not only to receive the reality once but to go on and on experiencing and absorbing the divine love which God himself describes so powerfully when he reminds us that, from the very beginning, he has called us by name:

You are mine and I am yours. You are my Beloved. On you my favour rests. I have moulded you in the depths of the earth and knitted you together in your mother's womb. I have carved you in the palms of my hands and hidden you in the shadow of my embrace. I look at you with infinite tenderness and care for you with a care more intimate than that of a mother for her child. I have counted every hair on your head and guided you at every step. Wherever you go, I go with you, and wherever you rest, I keep watch. I will give you food that will satisfy all your hunger, and drink that will quench all your thirst. I will not hide my face from you. You know me as your own as I know you as my own. You belong to me… Wherever you are I will be. Nothing will ever separate us. We are one. [1]

When we know ourselves loved by God like that, slowly but surely, by the grace of God's Spirit, our hearts are stirred. We love in return—as we observed at the beginning of the first section of this book.

Unlike Mary of Bethany, when our hearts have been warmed by the divine love, we cannot anoint the head or wash the feet of Jesus. What we can do, though, is to listen in the hushed and hidden places of our heart—listen to his word, even listen to his longings, listen to his heartbeat. As we listen, Jesus' parable of the sheep and the goats may well be brought to our awareness:

'When he finally arrives, blazing in beauty and all his angels with him, the Son of Man will take his place on his glorious throne. Then all the nations will be arranged before him and he will sort the people out, much as a shepherd sorts out sheep and goats, putting sheep to his right and goats to his left.

'Then the King will say to those on his right, "Enter, you who are blessed by my Father! Take what's coming to you in this kingdom. It's been ready for you since the world's foundation. And here's why:

I was hungry and you fed me,

I was thirsty and you gave me a drink,

I was homeless and you gave me a room,

I was shivering and you gave me clothes,

I was sick and you stopped to visit,

I was in prison and you came to me."

'Then those "sheep" are going to say, "Master, what are you talking about? When did we ever see you hungry and feed you, thirsty and give you a drink? And when did we ever see you sick or in prison and come to you?" Then the King will say, "I'm telling the solemn truth: Whenever you did one of these things to someone overlooked or ignored, that was me—you did it to me."'

MATTHEW 25:31–40 (THE MESSAGE)

As we ponder this passage, God's message becomes inescapably clear. Jean Vanier sums it up memorably when he reminds us that the clear call of Christ to some of us is to leave everything—even to become beggars of compassion like St Francis of Assisi. He invites others to leave their familiar surroundings so that they can more effectively share their lives with the poor and the weak. Still others he calls to invite into their hearts and homes an elderly, lonely neighbour or a disabled child.

As we see through parables like the good Samaritan, Jesus calls each of us to incarnate his compassion wherever we find ourselves. Startlingly and memorably, Jean Vanier claims that the poor and the weak with whom he has worked so faithfully for so many years are the people who have revealed to him 'the great secret of Jesus'. The secret is this. If we wish to follow him, instead of trying to climb the ladder of success and power, becoming more and more important, impressive and powerful, we should walk *down* the ladder to meet and greet and journey alongside those who are broken and in pain: people who are out of work, the ever-increasing number in our society who are caught up in the world of drugs, those who were emotionally wounded when they were young, people recently out of prison, those who are oppressed because of the colour of their skin, the lonely and the destitute, to name but a few.

When the call came to me to leave not only the cottage that I loved but my country, my culture and my grown-up children, my reaction was very mixed. I was in touch with awe. I was also in touch with excitement. The predominant feeling, though, was one of fear. Would I be able to cope? My eventual 'Yes' to God was whispered only after a painful and prolonged struggle. Others have been prepared to utter a more resounding 'Yes' than my rather pathetic whisper. The prayers in this section of the book begin with God's plaintive, persistent call. They continue by reflecting the joy and the pain, the anticipation and the fear with which Christians down the ages have expressed their willingness and readiness to serve God by serving people—whether at home or in distant lands.

LOVING HEART

Will you be the one who will serve me intensely?
Will you listen to the heart cries of your neighbour
    after everyone else has walked away…?
Will you be the one who stays up longest to hear his woeful story?
Will you be the one to look longest
    for some trace of me in the desolate,
    the derelict,
    the alcoholic?
Will you try to find some resemblance of the Father
    in the one who slanders you?
Will you be the one to keep on loving
    even when the love is unrequited?
Will you ask others in to share your meal
    when there is no assurance of your next meal?
Will you go forth and console others
    when your own need of consolation is beyond tears?
Will you forgive others
    even though others refuse to forgive you?
Care when no one cares;
    love when no one loves;
    fill others from your own emptiness?
Could you rather pardon than be pardoned;
    could you rather like than be liked;
    love rather than be loved?
Understand rather than be understood?
Can you accept insult
    and give forth praise in exchange…
    take ridicule and give forth understanding in exchange?
Will you listen attentively
    even though your own problems are thundering in your heart?
Will you speak lovingly of my will
    even when it has crushed you?
Then, surrendered heart,
minister to my people in pure love.

JOAN HUTSON [2]

SAYING YES

This prayer was written after meditating on the annunciation, sitting with the Holy Trinity in the heavenly places and contemplating a world hurtling to destruction.

Mary,
like clay in the potter's hands,
soft, malleable, yielding,
you inspire me to say yes.

Holy Trinity,
like birds brooding over their young,
watching, waiting, wondering,
bring to birth my yes.

Father,
like a lover longing for the loved one,
wooing, giving, sacrificing,
strengthen my yes.

Jesus,
Father's delight, Father's darling,
a foetus in a woman's womb,
give me the grace to say yes.

Holy Spirit,
co-Creator of the universe,
energy flowing from the Father,
empower me to say yes.

Mary,
still the same
yet strangely different,
nurturing the Saviour-seed,

carrying your secret wherever you go,
teach me to say yes—
   not one yes
     but a thousand yeses
       a new yes
         with every new morning
           and every turn of the road
that I, too, may become part of this mystery:
  our Master's plan
    for the salvation of the world.

IJH

MY NEW MISSION

Going, not in the spring-time of my years
   but in the late summer.
Ripened, with a wrinkle here and there
   and the odd grey hair!
Going, not with the daring of youth
   but with the calm of mid life…
In touch with the weaknesses,
   aware of the strengths.
Going, not with the idealism of the young
   but bringing the realism of experience…
Shaped by life's dyings,
   by her life-giving loves.
I need your compassion, Lord, to go with
   a listening, trusting, feeling heart,
     receptive, patient, a love filled with passion…
       compassion for your people.
Going, knowing I come only with God and me.
Coming, to discover their God and them.

BARBARA CAMERON [3]

DEDICATION

This was written as a result of meditating on a number of passages
from Matthew's Gospel in succession: Matthew 25:31–46; Jesus'
clear statement, 'The Son of Man is going to be betrayed and
crucified' (26:2) and the anointing at Bethany (26:6–13).

Suffering one,
   I hold to you all that I have
      and all that I am
   that your love would flow, not just into me
      but through me
   to caress and bless
      the lives of others.
   For, beloved Bridegroom
      I love you
      and would minister to you
      if I could.
      I do it in the only way I know—
      by ministering to others
      in your name.

Loved one,
   I receive your offering of love,
      your dedication of self;
   you will watch, with awe, while I break you
      and use you
   by distributing you in far-flung places.
   You have only to trust
      and rest
   and you will be blessed
   and become an ever-increasing blessing,
   reaping a rich harvest
      for my kingdom.

IJH

Lord,
I know not what I ought to ask of you.
You only know what I need.
You know me better than I know myself...
Teach me to pray.
Pray yourself in me.

ARCHBISHOP FRANÇOIS FÉNELON (1651–1715)

JESUS

This prayer was written as a result of meditating on the temptations of Jesus in the wilderness and becoming acutely aware of his youthfulness, yet his sense of purpose and direction.

Jesus,
young,
strong,
sensitive,
powerful
God-man.
Teach me to live as you lived:
with only one desire—
to be God's person
   at God's moment
      in the right place at the right time
      poised
         like an athlete waiting for
         the starting gun,
ready to flex every nerve and muscle
   until the race is won.

LJH

A PRAYER OF ABANDONMENT

Father, I abandon myself into your hands;
   do with me what you will.
Whatever you may do, I accept all.
Let only your will be done in me,
   and in all your creatures—
   I wish no more than this, O Lord.
Into your hands I commend my soul;
   I offer it to you with all the love of my heart,
   for I love you, Lord, and so need to give myself,
   to surrender myself into your hands without reserve,
   and with boundless confidence,
   for you are my Father.

CHARLES DE FOUCAULD (1858–1916)

LOST AND FOUND

This was written as a result of meditating on the parables about
'lost things'—lost coin, lost sheep, lost sons—from Luke 15.

Beloved,

For searching for me
as the Middle Eastern woman
   searched for her silver coin
I adore you.
For leaving the splendours of heaven
to lift me from the thicket
I honour you.
For turning me
   from an alien
      into a member of God's family
I give you heartfelt praise.

Father,

For sparing your Son
I worship you.
For giving me the grace to see
I give you praise.
For impressing your truths on me
    as thumbs make their imprint on soft clay
I give you humble and heartfelt thanks
    and offer you
        all that I am
            all that I have
                all that I can become
for you to use
as you choose
from now
    and into eternity.

LJH

TURN ME, LORD

One of the prayers that I pray most regularly is a short one
popularized by Ignatius of Loyola. One variation of it is 'Turn my
whole being to your praise and service.' While praying this prayer
on one occasion, I found myself adding a longer prayer of my own.

Whatever it costs, Beloved,
turn my whole being to your praise and service,
keep me from becoming blind or deaf,
    stupid or cunning—
        limited.
Rather, cause me to abandon all to you.
For, at the deepest level of my being,
heart-hunger gives rise to a heart-cry:

'Don't ask me to leave you
nor to refrain from following after you.
Where you go,
I will go…'

Here and now,
I offer to you
all that I have
and all that I am.
If it means accepting abuse or poverty
so be it.
I commit myself to you
'for better, for worse,
for richer, for poorer,
in sickness and in health',
accepting all, whatever you choose to send;
using all,
welcoming all,
knowing that it comes giftwrapped
with love from you—
echoing those truths penned by Ramon Lull:
'What is the greatest darkness?
The absence of my Beloved.
And what is the greatest light?
The presence of my Beloved.'

LJH

CALLED

I know
that I am called.
The message was quite clear
and yet I cannot see
the how, the why.

I feel so small, so weak,
so ill equipped
for such a task.
And yet I am prepared
to say my yes
and undertake the risk
and enter the unknown,
responding to the call.
Trustfully treading my way,
the only one
that leads to life—
to him.

HENRY ROHR[4]

LIKE JESUS

Lord Jesus, teach me to be generous,
to serve you as you deserve to be served;
to give and not to count the cost;
to fight and not to heed the wounds;
to toil and not to seek for rest;
to labour and to ask for no reward,
save that of knowing that I do your holy will.

IGNATIUS OF LOYOLA (1491–1556)

ALL IS OF YOU

Jesus, may all that is you flow into me,
may your body and blood be my food and drink.
May your passion and death be my strength and life.
Jesus, with you by my side enough has been given.
May the shelter I seek be the shadow of your cross.
Let me not run from the love which you offer,
but hold me safe from the forces of evil.
On each of my dyings shed your light and love.
Keep calling me until that day comes
when, with your saints, I may praise you for ever.

And Jesus, while I walk this earth,
remind me often
that my resources do not come from me,
they simply flow through me.
You are the giver,
I am simply the receptacle.
This awareness excites,
    strengthens,
        and encourages me.
The realization that I am never the source
of an insight,
    a book,
        or an inspiration
humbles me.
It challenges me to abide,
        to wait,
        to listen,
for all
    all
    all—
    is of you.

VERSE 1, 'THE SOUL OF CHRIST', IGNATIUS OF LOYOLA;
REMAINING LINES, LJH

THE BODY OF CHRIST

Whenever I pray this prayer, my mind goes to the church where members of the St Egidio Community in Rome meet to pray. There, hanging on the wall, is a crucifix that seemed to draw me to itself. The body of Christ has no arms and no legs. When I asked a member of the community why it hung there, he said, 'We hang it here to remind us that, today, Christ has no hands but our hands and no feet but our feet.'

Lord Jesus, I give you my hands to do your work,
I give you my feet to go your way,
I give you my eyes to see as you do,
I give you my tongue to speak your words.
I give you my mind that you may think in me,
I give you my spirit that you may pray in me.
Above all, I give you my heart
that you may love in me your Father and all mankind.
I give you my whole self that you may grow in me so that
    it is you, Lord, Jesus,
who live and work and pray in me.

THE GRAIL PRAYER[5]

DESERT FERTILITY

Spirit of Life,
    hover over me, breathe life into me, empower me,
bring to birth the seeds of love, and peace, and compassion
    growing in me.
Make me fertile with the seeds of the fruits of the Spirit:
    nourish them, nurture them, ripen them into fruitfulness.
Pour out your Spirit on the gifts, your gifts, you have
    given me that I may prophesy and dream dreams and see
    visions as you promised.

Breathe life into me in abundance,
   and let it flow from me abundantly.
Spirit of Life,
   flow through me powerfully, vitally,
   that my presence to others may always be life-giving.
   Continue to be born in me, to bring me to birth
   every day, increasing my capacity for love,
   for peace, for compassion, for abundance,
   for gratitude, for living life
   and bringing life to others.

BARBARA CAMERON[6]

FOR YOU ALONE

Dear Lord and Saviour, Jesus Christ,
I hold up all my weakness to your strength,
my failure to your faithfulness,
my sinfulness to your perfection,
my loneliness to your compassion,
my little pains to your great agony on the cross.

I pray that you will cleanse me,
   strengthen me,
      guide me,
so that in all ways my life may be lived
as you would have it lived,
without cowardice,
and for you alone.
Show me how to live in true humility,
   true contrition
      and true love.

PRINTED ON A PRAYER CARD WITH THE INITIALS MS

THE REFUGEE

At harvest time in the part of Cyprus where I lived, fieldmice and
rats were hounded from their homes by harvesters. Since we lived
in the corner of a field, they seemed to take a liking to our home
and garden at that time of year. The task of controlling them was
onerous and sometimes distressing. The rat I describe seemed
menacing until I watched it die!

Diligent harvesters demolished its home;
it came seeking a niche in mine,
but its behaviour proved unacceptable.
It cut the cable of my modem with its scissor-sharp teeth,
it pierced the hose linking the washing machine
   to the water supply
and flooded the floor.
I set up a witch-hunt for it,
fed it with dishes full of pretty poison.
I determined to drive it from my home
by killing it.

Tonight it lay listless on the patio;
its little paws were bleeding.
It washed its face for the last time—
in blood.
Then it crept into a corner to hide—to die.
The bloodstained paw marks on the patio stared up at me,
persuading me that the little creature, now so harmless,
   must be hurting.
I heard the Beloved's voice reminding me
that the Father cares about each falling sparrow,
and my heart was suddenly sorrowful.
I had deliberately killed one of God's creatures.

Maybe rats have to be exterminated, Lord,
but what about those other refugees,
the ones I watched on television today
running helplessly from their homes,
clutching only one bundle of belongings?
By my negligence
and dismissal of their plight,
by keeping them out of my heart and home
because their behaviour might not be acceptable,
am I, by any chance, killing them too?

May I feel the pain of the displaced.
May it prompt me to be to them
what you would have me be,
dear Light of the world.

LJH

YOURS

Majestic Sovereign, timeless wisdom,
your kindness melts my hard, cold soul.
Handsome lover, selfless giver,
your beauty fills my dull, sad eyes.
I am yours, you made me,
I am yours, you called me,
I am yours, you saved me,
I am yours, you loved me,
I will never leave your presence.
Give me death, give me life,
Give me sickness, give me health,
Give me honour, give me shame,
Give me weakness, give me strength,
I will have whatever you give.

TERESA OF AVILA (1515–82)

THE FRAGRANCE OF CHRIST

Dear Jesus,
help me to spread your fragrance
everywhere I go.
Flood my soul with your spirit and life.
Penetrate and possess my whole being so utterly
that my life may only be a radiance of yours.
Shine through me,
and so be in me,
that every soul I come in contact with
may feel your presence.
Let them look up and see
no longer me but only Jesus.
Stay with me,
and then I shall begin to shine
as you shine,
so to shine as to be a light to others;
the light, O Jesus,
will be all from you,
none of it will be mine;
it will be you shining on others through me.
Let me praise you in the way you love best
by shining on those around me.
Let me preach you,
not by words only,
but by the catching force of example,
the evident fullness
of the love my heart bears to you.

MOTHER TERESA OF CALCUTTA (1910–97)[7]

JESUS MY LEADER

Jesus,
I see you as you were as a youth
and a young leader:
strong, vigorous, full of integrity,
with the best interests of people at heart,
with the burning desire to make life better
for everyone
so that all could come into your kingdom.
I want to follow you, Lord.
I want to take you as my leader.
I want to improve the lot
of those who are being exploited.
Lead me.
Guide our steps
to that place where we can be most effective
for you in reaching out to others.

Holy Spirit,
thank you for opening my eyes to see Jesus as he really is:
a person with a cutting edge.
Change me into his likeness
that I may be a sharp tool in his hands
whatever it costs.
Continue to open my eyes until I see him
as he really is.

IJH

OPEN TO GOD

Prise open my fingers,
  O God,
that nothing:
  my cottage
    my country
      my culture
and no one:
  my children
    my companions
      my confidantes
may keep me
  from being radically open
    to you
or prevent me from
  saying yes to you.

LJH

There will be times when you will not see the immediate way ahead. You may be filled with panic, wanting to avoid what could be a disastrous step. Remember that you do not always need to see the road ahead. It is sufficient, for the moment, to see me.

When the time is right for a choice to be made, you will know and I will assist you through it. Until that time be sure that merely keeping close to me guarantees your moving in the right direction, despite questions and doubts raging in your mind.

JOHN WOOLLEY [8]

A PRAYER OF ST IGNATIUS

When I copied this prayer into my journal, I was overwhelmed by
the privilege of being handpicked by God to serve him and help to
usher in his kingdom.

Eternal Lord,
    King of all creation…
        I am moved by your grace
            to offer myself to you
            and your work.
I deeply desire to be with you
    in accepting all wrongs,
        all abuse,
            all poverty—
            actual and spiritual—
and I deliberately choose this
    if it is for your greater service
        and praise.

If you,
    my Lord and King,
        would so call
            and choose me,
then take and receive me
    into such a way of life.

GOING WITH GOD

The road stretches out
    and as I take
    one step,
and two,
    the road moves on.

No end in sight.
   Just new
   horizons.
But you are there,
   taking the steps
   as I take them.
   Sharing
   the adventure.
Lord, it's risky,
there's so much space.
   But the
real shelter is not the
   walls I build.
It's in you.

EDDIE ASKEW [9]

I wrote the following prayer after meditating on the visit of the magi and the phrase from the hymn, 'the gold of obedience'. Jesus himself seemed to be the model of obedience in that he took as his life's motto, 'I have come to do your will, O God.' I found myself wanting to echo that motto.

Grant, O Lord,
that I may be willing to go where you lead,
to endure hardships for the sake of your kingdom,
to hold lightly to greatness or littleness.
May my heart always prompt me
to seek your face,
Beloved One.

LJH

ANIMA CHRISTI

Soul of Christ, sanctify me
Body of Christ, save me
Blood of Christ, inebriate me
Water from the side of Christ, wash me
Passion of Christ, strengthen me
O good Jesus, hear me
Within your wounds hide me
Permit me not to be separated from thee
From the wicked foe defend me
At the hour of my death call me
And bid me come to thee
That with thy saints I may praise thee
For ever and ever. Amen

FROM THE 14TH CENTURY

UNBOUNDED LOVE

When I pray this prayer, which is my adaptation of a prayer written
by Charles Simeon, I often have in my mind one of the claims of
Mary Euphrasia Pelletier: 'Our work is God's work, and God will
protect it.'[10]

What is before us,
    we know not,
    whether we shall live or die;
but this we know,
    that all things are ordered and sure.
Everything is ordered,
    with unerring wisdom
    and unbounded love,
    by you, our God,
you who are love.

Grant us in all things
   to see your hand;
   through Jesus Christ our Lord.

LJH

THE STRUGGLE

I once watched a fly fall off my bedside table into a spider's web and straight into the clutches of a spider. It reminded me of the way I can still be ensnared by the seeming attractions of the world. Although the people I most admire are those who have given up everything for the sake of the kingdom, as a missionary working overseas I occasionally caught myself longing for a more spacious house, a fixed salary rather than having to raise support, a sense of belonging (Christianly and culturally), and acceptance (rather than living under the suspicion of the secret police). I sometimes envied those whose conscience allowed them to serve Christ and live a comfortable, middle-class lifestyle. Such self-awareness gave rise to this prayer.

Jesus,
Beloved,
I feel as though a tug of war is going on inside me.
I feel drawn by you and your lifestyle,
yet pulled away by the lure of riches and status,
honour and applause.
Give me the grace to say yes.

Father,
you didn't cling to your one and only Son,
you gave him up—
for me.

Enchant me over and over again,
   that my attachment to you
      may loosen my grip
         on life's seeming treasures
and set me free
to be the person
you always intended me to be.

LJH

SHOW YOURSELF TO ME, LORD

I wrote this prayer while meditating on Jesus' appearance to
Thomas, during a retreat on St Thomas' Day 1995. The prayer was
inspired by Michael Cockett's song 'Show yourself to me, Lord'.

On this special day, Lord God,
I long to see you, as Thomas saw you:
   the love in your eyes,
      the acceptance in your face,
         the warmth of your smile.
 'My child,' you said, 'if you would see me,
   gaze at my world,
      look at my people,
         reach out to my poor.'

On this special day, dear Lord,
I long to hear you, as Thomas heard you:
   the kindness in your voice,
      the invitation to draw near,
         the lack of condemnation.
 'My child,' you said, 'if you would hear me,
   hearken to the hungry,
      listen to the poor,
         hear the cries of those ravaged by war.'

On this special day, dear Lord,
I long to touch you, as Thomas touched you.
   I long, lovingly, to finger your wounds,
      to caress your feet,
         to hold and be held.
 'My child,' you said, 'if you would touch me,
    hold the hopeless,
       reach out to the rejected,
          nurse the sick in body, mind and spirit.
And rest assured that
inasmuch as you have seen, heard and touched my poor ones,
you have seen, heard and touched me.'

IJH

WE REST ON THEE

I first heard this prayer sung as a hymn on the film *Through Gates of Splendour*—the story of the martyrdom of missionaries who had gone to work among the Auca Indians in South America. The film inspired me and the hymn haunted me. My husband and I chose it as one of our wedding hymns. I echo it more and more as I go on in the Christian life.

'We rest on thee', our shield and our defender;
   We go not forth alone against the foe;
Strong in thy strength, safe in thy keeping tender
   'We rest on thee, and in thy name we go.'

Yea, 'in thy name', O Captain of salvation!
   In thy dear name, all other names above;
Jesus our righteousness, our sure foundation,
   Our Prince of glory and our King of love.

We go in faith, our own great weakness feeling,
    And needing more each day thy grace to know;
Yet from our hearts a song of triumph pealing:
    'We rest on thee, and in thy name we go.'

'We rest on thee', our shield and our defender,
    Thine is the battle; thine shall be the praise
When passing through the gates of pearly splendour,
    Victors, we rest, with thee through endless days.

EDITH GILLING CHERRY (1872–97)

TAKE, LORD, AND RECEIVE

Take, Lord,
    and receive all my liberty,
    my memory, my understanding
    and my entire will—
    all that I have and possess.

    You have given all to me,
    to you, Lord, I return it.

    All is yours;
    do with it what you will.

    Give me only your love
    and your grace,
    that is enough for me.

FROM *THE SPIRITUAL EXERCISES OF ST IGNATIUS*

✜

When times are tough

Loving God leads to loving the world.
Loving God passionately leads to loving the world passionately.
Hoping in God is hoping for the salvation of the world.

I often say to myself that… God must feel very much alone: for is there anyone besides God who believes in the salvation of the world? God seeks among us sons and daughters who resemble him enough, who love the world enough that he could send them into the world to save it.

So writes Louis Evely in *The Christian Spirit*.[1] Those who watch the news on television or Internet, or read the newspapers regularly, know that engaging with the world is far from easy. Jesus himself warned his listeners that loving the world would be costly. 'In this world you will have trouble,' he prophesied (John 16:33).

The disciples discovered the accuracy of this warning while Jesus was still with them. As Mark recalls, there were occasions when 'so many people were coming and going that [Jesus and the disciples] did not even have a chance to eat' (Mark 6:31). After Jesus' death, problems assailed the disciples at every twist and turn of the road, as a glance at the Acts of the Apostles reminds us. In Acts 4, for example, we see Peter and John thrilling the crowds but enraging the temple guards with their teaching. They are arrested but, after spending time in prison, they emerge to find an even bigger crowd waiting for them: 'the number of men grew to about five thousand' (v. 4). They are then arrested by the Sadducees. In chapter 7, Stephen similarly is seized, harassed and stoned. Meanwhile, Saul is channelling all his energy and in-genuity into seeking to eliminate the infant church.

Recalling Stephen's martyrdom, Luke puts the situation graphically:

On that day a great persecution broke out against the church at Jerusalem, and all except the apostles were scattered throughout Judea and Samaria. Godly men buried Stephen and mourned deeply for him. But Saul began to destroy the church. Going from house to house, he dragged off men and women and put them in prison.

ACTS 8:1–3

After his own amazing conversion to Christ, Paul also testifies to the truth of Jesus' prophecy, 'In the world you will have trouble.'

I have… been in prison… and been exposed to death again and again. Five times I received from the Jews the forty lashes minus one. Three times I was beaten with rods, once I was stoned, three times I was shipwrecked, I spent a night and a day in the open sea… I have been in danger from rivers, in danger from bandits, in danger from my own countrymen, in danger from Gentiles; in danger in the city, in danger in the country, in danger at sea; and in danger from false brothers. I have laboured and toiled and have often gone without sleep; I have known hunger and thirst and have often gone without food; I have been cold and naked. Besides everything else, I face daily the pressure of my concern for all the churches. Who is weak, and I do not feel weak? Who is led into sin, and I do not inwardly burn? … In Damascus the governor under King Aretas had the city of the Damascenes guarded in order to arrest me. But I was lowered in a basket from a window in the wall and slipped through his hands.

2 CORINTHIANS 11:23–33

Yes, the cost of catching Christ's compassion for the world is incalculable. The mature, mellowed Peter puts it this way: 'Dear friends, do not be surprised at the painful trial you are suffering, as though something strange were happening to you. But rejoice that you participate in the sufferings of Christ, so that you may be overjoyed when his glory is revealed' (1 Peter 4:12–13).

Here, surely, the ageing apostle is building on the Beatitudes (Matthew 5)? In *Praying the Kingdom*, Charles Elliott suggests that, when we ponder these powerful sayings of Jesus, we should replace the word 'blessed' with the phrase, 'in the right place...'

You are in the right place when...
You are poor in spirit.
You mourn.
You hunger and thirst for righteousness.
You are merciful.
You are persecuted.
You become a peacemaker.[2]

Or, to use Eugene Peterson's punchy paraphrase, you are in the right place when... 'you're at the end of your rope... you feel you've lost what is most dear to you... you've worked up a good appetite for God... you care... you can show people how to cooperate instead of compete or fight... your commitment to God provokes persecution' (*THE MESSAGE*).

My role when I first wrote this book was to listen to, lead retreats for and pray for Christians who felt called by God to live overseas. Many of them serve God in some of the world's toughest places. When I was giving birth to this book, I lived overseas too. Although I lived in a beautiful country that I love, and although my husband and I relished our home, I frequently found that the going was tough. Loneliness often gnawed at my heart. Stripped of the resources I took for granted in the homeland, helplessness often mocked me. Then there was the language barrier. Since I never learned the language spoken by the people in my village, I frequently felt an alien—a stranger in the place I called 'home'.

At the same time, though, I felt loved by many of my neighbours and I was curiously content. 'You sparkle,' one person observed on one occasion. Was that because I knew that I was in the place to which God had called us? Or was it because, deep down, I knew that we were in the place where God wanted us to be at that time? I was also well aware that the problems and fears that I faced were but tiny hillocks compared with the mountain-range of problems that troubled many of my friends: some were living in war-torn countries, some were locked in conflict with their colleagues, some were compelled to live so simply that they had almost forgotten what it meant to live comfortably.

Most of the prayers that appear in this section of *Embracing God's World* have been penned by such people: God's unsung heroes and heroines who have experiential knowledge of Jesus' warning, 'In the world you shall have trouble'. How I long that each person who dips into this book could meet those who wrote these prayers. Many of them are a very real inspiration—'blessed' because, though the going continues to be tough, they are in the right place at the right time and they are aware of that fact.

There are times when even the most courageous of us feels like giving up. God knows this. At such times, he so often speaks into our situation with sensitivity and love—pouring strength into those areas of our life where all strength and energy seem to have been sapped. That is why, in this section in particular, I make it plain that true prayer is two-way. We speak to God; God responds. Or God speaks to us and we respond. In other words, while we are praying, God is listening, loving and responding to us.

MY HEART IS READY

This prayer was written when reflecting on a car accident in which
I was involved but, miraculously, not hurt.

You, Lord, have been
Light in my darkness,
Hope in my despair,
Love in my loneliness;
the Protector who watched over me
    when danger engulfed me,
the Lifegiver who snatched me
    from the jaws of death,
the Intercessor who prayed
    that my faith and resolve
        might not fail,
the Joy-giver who pierced and scattered
    the dark clouds of oppression,
my security when the path before me
    seemed like sinking sand.
So my heart is ready,
yes, my heart is ready
to worship
and adore
you, the Holy One
    to whom I may speak
        as I would speak with a friend.

LJH

On the day I wrote this prayer, I read the following in John
Woolley's inspiring book *I Am With You*:

You will be aware of much darkness, and of forces dedicated to ob-
structing your climb towards the heavenly sphere… Love in creativity
means that I am never remote from the inevitable heartaches of my
children… or, of course from your heartache.[3]

SADNESS AND JOY

Your grief will turn to joy.
JOHN 16:20 (NIV)

The agonising periods of existence which would almost make you lose your hold on me can serve a very relevant purpose for you... otherwise I would not permit them. Pain is the raw material from which you can be made a soul increasingly sensitive to my love's existence.
JOHN WOOLLEY [4]

GOD'S LOVE WILL TRIUMPH

Life's pain and sorrows,
allowed within my purposes of love,
are constantly used to create
what is ultimately noble and strong
and of the heavenly sphere.
They thus give deeper meaning
to the great miracle of existence itself...
the miracle that *I am*,
and that this is a universe
in which my love will triumph.
JOHN WOOLLEY [5]

AT THE END OF MY TETHER

The next prayer was written while I was still trying to recover from the shock of a car accident. I turn to this prayer sometimes when I read of people being involved in road accidents. Although they may emerge physically unharmed, the almost inevitable emotional trauma can cause havoc for many months.

Last night, Lord, I came to the end of my tether.
Four months of modern hassles finally wore me down.
The terror of travelling left my nerves frayed.
The frustration of communicating with people who neither act
    nor answer
    persuaded me that I can no longer cope.
Discovering all the things we'd left behind left me disappointed,
    despairing and angry.
The realization that I won't now be seeing my family next month
    gave rise to inconsolable grief.
Suddenly an inner dam burst.
Tears streamed relentlessly down my face,
tears that could not be controlled,
tears that flowed from a deeply damaged spirit.

I let them come;
they turned to sobs.

My neck ached.
My back ached.
My hand ached.
Most of all my heart ached.

I sat under the stars
and wished I had died in the car crash.
My eyes drank in the majesty
but it could not touch my now bleeding heart.

I called to you, Beloved,
persistently:
 'Jesus, Je-sus, JE-SUS!'
You seemed not to come—
    at least, not in a felt way.
But I knew you understood.

I saw you stumbling along the Via Dolorosa,
unable to cope.
I saw you fall beneath the weight of the cross,
or was it beneath the self-centredness of the world?
I heard you scream in Gethsemane:
 'Father, take this cup from me now...'
And I heard your fiat
    your Yes
    your:
    'Not my will
    but yours
        be done.'

When I woke
you were there
beside me,
the tender one.
You held me in a memorable, momentary, motherly embrace.
I mourned that I had left so many books behind:
'Read my other book,' you whispered.
The sunshine's slender fingers beckoned me out of my tent.
I parked my chair in a pool of sunlight.
The hard, parched, barren earth,
    the prickly pine needles,
    the liberal studding of stones,
    aptly summed up the state of my soul.
But before I could be ashamed
one autumn crocus captured my attention.
Its purple petals had parted in the sun.
It stood with palms upturned to the towering pine trees.
It revelled in the sun's rays.
Its openness revealed six sepals covered in pollen.
I gasped.
'My gift,' you whispered.
I gazed at this your gift.

You whispered again.
'Just as your eyes focus,
    not on the barrenness,
    nor on the hardness
    of the terrain,
    but on the beauty before you—
    the delicate delights of one small flower
    that has pushed its way through many obstacles—
    so my eye focuses
    not on your failure
    but on my desire
    that your whole being
    should be turned
    to my honour and glory.
    I honour you for that.
    I hear your heartache and I care.
    I see your exhaustion and I weep.
    I am praying that your faith will not fail,
    that your resolve will be strengthened and not weakened,
    that you would fix your gaze on me,
    the author and finisher of your faith journey.
    I delight to hear that hymn
    rising from the place of your woundedness:
    'I know that, Redeemer God, you live
    and that you will stand on the latter day
    upon the earth,
    and though worms destroy this body
    yet in my flesh
    I shall see God,
    my own beloved Redeemer God.'

So grant me the grace
to go on going on bearing hardships for the sake of the gospel:
whether these hardships be the perplexities of the
    fast-changing world,

the discouragement that comes through sowing precious seed
    in untilled soil,
or wherever.
Take me where you will.
Do with me what you will.
Use me or not as you will.
I am yours.
You are mine.
That is the only certainty in this unsettled time.
It is enough.

LJH

KEEP YOUR HAND IN MINE

You know that all the qualities you see in me
are available to you…
Be sure that your hand is firmly in mine…
I know that in your heart
is that longing to know me more perfectly.
I honour that longing,
and that is why you are sure of my patience
in all your sufferings.

JOHN WOOLLEY[6]

WHAT IF…?

Many Christians working overseas find themselves in war zones or
facing the threat of the outbreak of war. This prayer was written when
waves of fear swept over me as I feared the worst on one occasion.

Rumblings of war…
What if we have to evacuate?
What if I have to leave my computer behind?

What if I have to abandon my books?
What if there's no time to say goodbye
to neighbours and friends?
What if...?

Worse.
What if there's no time to evacuate?
What if they forget to warn us
of the need to flee?
What if food supplies run out?
What if our home is invaded?
What if...?

Like those rumblings of war,
storm clouds gather over the mountain range this morning,
Lord,
a threatening, menacing mass of steel grey.
Yet, already they're being dispersed by the rising sun
while those that remain are being tinged with pink and purple
on the underside.
'Whatever befalls, I'll be there,' you whisper,
'turning your grief to glory.'

My eyes turn from the sky to the soil.
There, perched on a tired-looking vine
sits a red-breasted robin
singing full-throttle to herald the day.
'Look at the birds,' you whisper—
'especially when you are anxious.'

LJH

THIS IS IT

The prayer that follows was written by a Christian worker in Lima, Peru. She recalls how, one night, she and her colleagues were woken at midnight by a very loud and frightening banging on their door.

This is it. It's them. They're at our door.
There's no escape. There's no going out.
Just wait for the moment.

I see the shadows on the glass.
I hear the knocking again.
I feel the need for protection.
I experience fear in the face of possible death.
In the dark I seek something to cover me,
    to protect my vulnerability.
And something outside of me to make God present to me,
    my cross, my rosary—something of God,
tangible with me in the 'hour of our death'.

Relief, in the sound of the landlord's step.
Relief, in their responses to his questions.
Relief, in the sight of disappearing shadows.
Relief, in the sisterly sharing of the moment.

God in the fear.
God in the relief.
God in the sharing.
'My hour had not yet come.'

BARBARA CAMERON

WAITING FOR GOD

Professor Kenneth Bailey gives us a glimpse of some of the struggles faced by Christians working overseas.

'I waited patiently for the Lord;
    He inclined unto me and heard my request.'

We know that the Psalmist sings such things, at least when he is
    feeling good.
Sometimes we feel that way too.
    Then there are other times when the sky is as brass above us
    and the earth is as iron under us;
and we cannot see the cloud the size of a man's hand rising
    over the sea.
So today,
we do not come in strength, but in weakness to be made strong:
not in wisdom, but in ignorance that we might learn your wisdom;
not in the fullness of your Spirit, but in emptiness to be filled.

We have seen your light shining brightly in the dark of night.
Its warmth and illumination have enriched us.
If it were not so, we would not have come to this place.
But you have called us to be a city on the hill.
    It is safer in the house, and quieter, and all there are friends.
The city on the hill is too exposed, Lord, and we are afraid:
    afraid that we will have to speak up, and will not know what
    to say;
    afraid that we will be identified and some harm will come to us;
    afraid that the things we hold most dearly will be subjected
    to mockery.
So—we fail to be a city on a hill.
    We are more like lamps flickering in the wind.
    Deliver us from fear of the wind;
    deliver us from retreating back into the house;

deliver us from fear lest our light go out—
    for you have kindled it and if we trust, we know it will
    shine through any storm.

'I waited for the Lord.'

Lord, we waited for your advent—and rejoiced in the light that
    came into the world in a manger.
We anticipated your cross and hoped for the resurrection—
    and found meaning in pain and hope in new life.
Now we await the coming of your Spirit.
Fill our lamps that we may with confidence shine
    in whatever place you send us:
    in office, store, market, study, home,
    classroom, hospital and city streets.
We pray for all those who seek peace and justice in this
    beloved, troubled land.
We pray for its leaders that they may have wisdom from above
    for all the daily decisions that they must make.
Bless us in the week ahead, that we may take each new
    disruption as an opportunity to seek new doors of ministry.
Fill our lamps, Lord, with the oil of your Spirit.
For only in your light do we see light
and without your Spirit, darkness descends upon us.

KENNETH BAILEY

LONELY HEART

I said, 'It is not good for man to be alone.' Yet, oh so many times I pull your friends from you, and you are painfully alone. Even surrounded by friends, you are an island and can only be talked to from distant shores. How often I have witnessed your heart crying, 'Oh friend, I cannot hold you close enough; you are still so very far away from me.'

That excruciating gap you must always sense, yet you are everlastingly trying to span it. You have learned that no arms will reach. I planted within you a homesickness for me. I did this to keep you striving for me. So many of you will exhaust yourselves trying to extinguish this flame of yearning with other hopeful fulfilments, while I stand by and watch you pass me by.

Lonely heart, stop running, stop searching. Recognize the aloneness you feel, look at it truthfully, honestly, and courageously and lovingly. Admit your hopelessness in alleviating it. Recognize your inability to escape it. Then, in hope, not despair, lift that lonely heart to me. Sometimes I will fill it with friends; sometimes only with the full understanding that I know and understand; sometimes with not even that assurance. Sometimes I will fill it with my absence.

Your inner being may passionately crave the heart of a fellow human being to talk to, to understand, and I may not grant what you ask. But I will give you the understanding of faith to believe that I'm aware of your loneliness, knowing that it is not time to dry your tears. Sometimes time must evaporate them. If a friend were to wipe them away too soon, you might not grow as I have planned for you. Let my awareness of what you suffer now in loneliness be your companion.

Offer it to me… I can use it to shape you! You, watch with me in Gethsemane… let the others sleep. With me, understand loneliness; with me, listen; with me, be healed.

JOAN HUTSON [7]

IN DARKNESS

In all those dark moments, O God,
grant that I may understand that it is you
who are painfully parting
the fibres of my being
in order to penetrate
to the very marrow of my substance…

TEILHARD DE CHARDIN (1881–1955)

WHEN DEPRESSED

You, O Christ,
who were despised and rejected by men,
know how I feel when,
by fault or failure,
I am cast into lonely pits of depression.
Draw me up from such despair
on the thin
yet cable-strong rope of prayer
to stand on 'this great roundabout—
the world'
and praise you.

LJH, ADAPTATION OF A PRAYER OF WILLIAM COWPER (1731–1800), 'THE JACKDAW'

✥

Going where it hurts

Listen my children:
listen to me.

I would speak to ears
   that will listen to me;
I would speak to eyes
   that will see as I see;
I would speak to lips
   that will say the words I give;
I would speak to hands
   that will be my compassion to the world;
I would speak to feet
   that will walk where I want to go;
I would speak to hearts
   that will beat only to love me.

Listen my children:
listen.

I speak from a war-torn country
   where brother fights brother;
I speak from the anguish of a young mother
   whose baby has been taken from her;
I speak in the old man hanging on to life
   by a thread;
I speak in the young woman for whose illness
   medicine has no cure;
I speak in the troubled heart,
   the mind filled with fear;

I speak in the howling of the wind,
   the thunder in the sky,
      the crash of a hurricane...
but I speak too in the rainbow;
in soft dewdrops;
in shafts of sunlight;
in stillness.
I speak in laughter;
I speak in a smile;
but most of all my children,
I speak in silence.
   So listen my children—
listen to me;
listen—listen...

SUE ASHDOWN

If we do what those words beg us to do, if we step off the treadmill from time to time, seek solitude and open the ears of our hearts to God, we will hear many voices. We may tune in to God's voice that finds myriad ways of whispering the healing message we all need to hear: 'I love you.' We will also almost certainly hear the plaintive cry of the sick and sorrowful, the lonely, the depressed and the oppressed. We can't go to them all. Neither is that our calling. We can go to some. We can pray for others.

In the still place that Sue Ashdown describes, God will fill us afresh with his love so that, when we go to his hurting ones, we will not go empty-handed. We will go with eyes full of his love, lips that speak words of wisdom, consolation or grace, hands and arms that express his tenderness and warmth.

And, of course, when we go, we visit not just a human, hurting person; we meet and touch Jesus himself. As he reminds us, in Eugene Peterson's paraphrase of Matthew 25:31–40:

'The Son of Man will take his place on his glorious throne. Then all the nations will be arranged before him and he will sort the people out, much

as a shepherd sorts out sheep and goats, putting sheep to his right and goats to his left.

'Then the King will say to those on his right, "Enter, you who are blessed by my Father! Take what's coming to you in this kingdom. It's been ready for you since the world's foundation. And here's why:

I was hungry and you fed me,

I was thirsty and you gave me a drink,

I was homeless and you gave me a room,

I was shivering and you gave me clothes,

I was sick and you stopped to visit,

I was in prison and you came to me."

'Then those "sheep" are going to say, "Master, what are you talking about? When did we ever see you hungry and feed you, thirsty and give you a drink? And when did we ever see you sick or in prison and come to you?" Then the King will say, "I'm telling the solemn truth: Whenever you did one of these things to someone overlooked or ignored, that was me—you did it to me."'

Sometimes, when we visit those who are hurting, we will not know what to say, what to do or how to pray. At such times, it can be a strange comfort simply to remind ourselves that God knows. As Sue Ashdown puts it, God 'knows each grain of sand, each blade of grass, each ant and spider that walks unseen by human eyes. God knows each breath we take, each thought we think—before we think it' (Psalm 139:2). 'Even the hairs on our heads are numbered' (Luke 12:7a).

HE KNOWS

A leaf falls to the ground:
a tiny flutter,
no sound.
   He knows.

A sparrow sheds a feather:
the slightest movement,
no noise.
   He knows.

A tiny spider curls and dies:
no trumpet call,
just nothing.
   He knows.

A lily bends and breaks in the wind:
no scream of pain,
just silence.
   He knows.

A heart lifted in joy:
but whom to tell,
just a smile.
   He knows.

A mind torn with pain:
only silence is heard,
no heart's cry.
   He knows.

A hand lifted in defence:
no justice felt,
just vulnerability.
   He knows.

A soul seeking to follow:
no perfection here,
just sin.
He knows.

A life longing to serve:
No unhindered walk,
but stumbling.
He knows.

A breath drawn in waiting:
no certainty for ease,
just obedience.
He knows.

A whisper from heart's depths:
no eloquent phrases,
just 'My Lord'.
He knows.
He knows.

SUE ASHDOWN

AN INSTRUMENT OF PEACE

Lord, make me an instrument of thy peace.
Where there is hatred, let me sow love.
Where there is injury, pardon.
Where there is discord, vision.
Where there is doubt, faith.
Where there is despair, hope.
Where there is darkness, light.
Where there is sadness, joy.
O divine Master,
grant that I may not so much seek to be consoled as to console;

to be understood as to understand;
to be loved, as to love;
for it is in giving that we receive,
it is in pardoning that we are pardoned,
and it is in dying that we are born to eternal life.

ATTRIBUTED TO FRANCIS OF ASSISI (1181–1226)

WHO COULD HAVE KNOWN?

Children are a gift from God and they give incredible joy—but they also bring unspeakable sorrow. In J. Neville Ward's book *Five for Sorrow, Ten for Joy*,[1] he reminds us of the occasion when Mary and Joseph 'lost' Jesus when he was just twelve years old. They found him three days later in the temple. Although he obediently returned to them, he was a different person, no longer needing them in the way he had appeared to need them before. Mary and Joseph had to let their child 'die' so that he could become the changed person they were now witnessing. This way, he would be free to love them without staying emotionally dependent on them. This 'letting go', this 'losing', can be frighteningly painful to parents. Most mothers of teenagers who are in the midst of those much-dreaded adolescent years can identify with Mary's pain and, I believe, could have written the following words.

Who could have known
   as I held that longed-for,
dreamt-of,
   suffered-for,
tiny
   'bundle of joy' close to my heart
that later
   she
would break it?

Who would have known
   that after all the joy,
the closeness,
   the oneness,
the watching,
   the holding,
the loving,
   would come
the anguish?

From heart's depths,
   from very roots of being
cries a voice
   rent with pain,
torn with the longings of love:
   a single cry
in desperation:
   'Help her—help me...'

Who could have known?

I have loved so much,
   planned so much,
longed so much,
   been one with.

Now part of myself
   is dying;
longing stretches out
   with arms to hold
and stays
   empty
as the cry comes again:
   'Help her—help me...'

Who could have known?

And from nowhere
   from everywhere,
from deep to deep
   comes with longing—
gently,
   lovingly,
God.

'I knew.
I have loved so,
planned so;
I am one with
My arms of love
hold her,
hold you.

I knew
I know.

   Come.'

SUE ASHDOWN

PARENTS IN PAIN

Father, my beautiful child
suffers—
she champions you
among her fellows
without compromise,
but it's her
they cull out,
cut down
and skin alive.

Once
I fought her battles for her;
I'm helpless now.
Such courage
makes me proud—
but when she bleeds,
I haemorrhage;
her rejection
aches in my spirit,
her loneliness
sobs in my heart,
and prayer is pain.

'Daughter,
I hear you.
My beautiful child
was crucified too.
His suffering
broke my heart.'

'This my Son whom I love… hated without reason.'

LINNET HINTON[2]

87

MY CHILD HAS GONE

Sue Ashdown writes: 'Friendship is about communication and forgiveness… In the case of our children, as they become young adults, it's also about two loving arms which never close in rejection but only round the newfound friend our child has become.'

She's gone, Lord,
the child I once knew—
and in her place—a woman
vulnerable—as all women are—
lacking polish,
needing assurance perhaps,
but nevertheless
a woman.

The pain of her birth into womanhood
was every bit as great
as the pain of her birth,
the more so perhaps, because of its
suddenness.
Then months of waiting,
of preparation.
Now—in a day—
separation.
She's gone.

My innocent daughter,
now initiated
into all the rites of womanhood
which by their very nature meant
I was not there.
Without me
her voyage of discovery
was begun.

She's gone—
and I must let her go.
Time now for painful rebuilding—
where innocence—now knowledge;
where wondering—now certainty;
where hesitancy—now assurance;
where childlike trust
now I must accept—
a woman's vulnerability.

Viewpoints considered—decisions made
—without me;
ideas formulated—carefully;
girlhood pushed back
—womanhood embraced
as she steps from my arms—
into his.
But she will discover
that womanhood's freedom is incomplete
and she may need my arms again.

So I will wait.
Not in desperation—but patiently,
for she may need me yet
as man needs man
and woman needs another woman—
and we will walk together, she and I
side by side.
For my child is gone
and in her place—
a woman.

Lord, give me the grace to wait.

SUE ASHDOWN

A WEDDING DAY

Weddings can be hard for clergy wives. While other couples enjoy one another's presence, the clergy wife often sits alone. If her marriage is going through a time of turbulence or if she is depressed for any reason, the wedding service can trigger the kind of pain being expressed by the clergy wife who breathed this prayer.

I sit alone.
Alone! Alone! Alone!
Mocked by the ceremony about to begin.
'It is not good for man to be alone',
said God.
And here I sit
alone.
I see couples cuddling
laughing
loving into each other's eyes.
They smile across the pews at me
alone,
pitiably, pitifully alone.
A few tears
squeeze from the beggar's bowl
of my aching heart
as those words of peace
slice through my soul
with the precision of a butcher's knife.
Once *we* made those vows.
But still I sit
alone.

'Marriage is a mosaic'
claims the preacher.
A mosaic.
My imagination plays with the image.

In offering one another the fragments that remain,
in placing one another, bit by bit,
on the ready plaster of God's love,
he makes us new.
Carefully he selects that which is offered,
piecing us together, bit by bit,
making us one.

'But tell them of the pain'
my heart cries.
Fragments are broken pieces.
You must offer little pieces of yourself
if you would form a good mosaic.
Tell them that the joins show—
ugly, dirty, unsightly seams
that unite the coloured pieces,
holding them together,
making of two persons, and many fragments,
one whole.

Tell them that it hurts
to be broken so small
to contribute to the picture.
Tell them that Love,
like a plastic frame,
holds their two loves together for always.
Tell them that when all hopes are dashed
into tiny, tiny pieces,
when all illusions explode
like an untimely bomb,
when their union lies in tatters
wasted on the ground,
he comes.
Patient.
Tender.
Skilful.

To gather up the fragments that remain,
to make of them a new picture,
one whole.

Lord, press me,
press us,
our few remaining fragments,
into the cement of your love
that we, too, may live
and hope
and love again.
Two 'I's
but one 'We'.

ANONYMOUS

LETTING GO

Sometimes, I find, the depth of my concern for a person can become an obstacle to my own prayer for that person. I have therefore found this a powerful and moving prayer to pray for some of the precious people in my life. I like the emphasis on letting God be God.

To a dear one about whom I have been concerned.

I behold the Christ in you.
I place you lovingly in the care of the Father.
I release you from my anxiety and concern.
I let go of my possessive hold on you.
I am willing to free you to follow the dictates
    of your indwelling Lord.
I am willing to free you to live your life
    according to your best light
    and understanding.

Husband, wife, child, friend—
I no longer try to force my ideas on you,
    my ways on you.
I lift my thoughts above you, above the personal level.
I see you as God sees you, a spiritual being,
    created in his image, and endowed with
    qualities and abilities that make you
    needed and important—not only to me
    but to God and his larger plan.
I do not bind you. I no longer believe that you
    do not have the understanding you need
    in order to meet life.
I bless you,
    I have faith in you,
        I behold Jesus in you.

AUTHOR UNKNOWN

A WOMEN'S LOCK-UP WARD

Reflecting on a visit to a psychiatric hospital

What breaks the people's hearts?
What tears their minds apart?
What is it that has the power
to reduce the creation in the image
    of the divine God
into a twisted heap of pain?

How is the human spirit healed?
How is the shattered mind restored?
    How is the power released
    that can free God's image
in the twisted heap of pain?

Can I be that power, Lord?
Can I love as you loved?
Touch as you touched?
Can I restore that which you created
    to what you created it to be?

Make me your instrument, Lord.
Hollow me and blow through me
the music that heals.

ZITA O'NEILL

GOD'S MIGRANTS

Linnet Hinton recalls that she wrote this prayer as a result of meeting in the home of Fijian Indians. 'We… represented a wide divergence of races and cultures. Two things united us: our common insecurity as new migrants and our shared love for the Lord Jesus Christ. Some had suffered persecution. As a recent arrival to Australia myself, I felt an enormous kinship with these special people who are so often disregarded by society.

They flee to us for refuge
from violent storms
of persecution, famine and war;
leaves stripped from their trees,
scattered by hurricanes of hatred and fear.
But you, Lord God, are master of the wind;
you ride upon the storm.
Not one of them is lost.

What they were before they are no more—
men of substance and repute perhaps,
now nobody—unrecognized, undervalued,
strangers in the world; struggling to survive
a painful transplant into foreign soil.

But these aliens, Lord,
are your chosen ones,
handpicked to follow you through suffering—
sprinkled with your blood,
sanctified by your Spirit,
people of destiny,
whom the world does not know
and is not worthy.

Thank you, Lord, for blowing them our way.
They may come empty-handed,
but their hearts are full of indestructible treasure,
true trophy of triumph in trial—
the knowledge of God.
They found you in fear-fuelled furnaces,
walked with you through death-dark valleys.
You were the one reality when all else dissolved—
the living God.
They knew you and were changed.

What stories they tell!
We warm our cold spirits at the fire of their faith
and reach out to touch you again.
Through this timely transfusion of costly new blood
you heal our anaemia, restore our energy
and bring fresh hope to a sick society.
O God, keep them from drifting
into a self-centred search for security
that would drain their vitality,
wither their witness and snuff out the light.
For they are your good gift to us
and we need them
desperately.

'God's elect, strangers in the world… scattered… chosen… of
God.'

LINNET HINTON [3]

FOR THE AFFLICTED

We bring before you, O Lord,
the troubles and perils of people and nations,
the sighing of prisoners and captives,
the sorrows of the bereaved,
the necessities of strangers,
the helplessness of the weak,
the despondency of the weary,
the failing powers of the aged.
O Lord, draw near to each
and show me how I may draw near
in your name
for the glory of Jesus.

LJH[4]

DOES ANYBODY CARE?

Linnet Hinton explains how she came to write this prayer: 'When this cruelly abused girl came to me for help, I felt helpless, out of my depth. Her condition challenged not only my love but my confidence in the ability of the Lord Jesus to salvage her.'

She sat there,
a spent shell—
empty voice speaking
of unspeakable things done to her,

At 20, disintegrating,
loosely labelled 'schizophrenic',
the fragments of her once three-dimensional self
laid out deadly flat,
glued and greyed with drugs.
Afraid to live, afraid to die.

Another casualty of a callous consumer society
where plastic people exist
to be used and abused for perverted pleasure,
factory-made duplicates—
anonymous, disposable.

But she is not biodegradable, nor recyclable,
finally absorbed by Mother Nature
into harmless oblivion.
Her soul is human, eternal,
handcrafted, individual,
designed with infinite potential for good—or ill.

A life blighted in bud
by high-tech barbarians
unable to appreciate the delicacy of divine artistry,
or the priceless blood of purity.
Employing violence, pressure-packed,
these vandals deface innocence with ugly graffiti
and viciously violate vulnerable virginity.

The city streets are littered
with social flotsam and jetsam such as she.
Garbage dumps of modernity,
heaped high with human waste,
lie at the very threshold of hell
where demonic cultures gather
to shred whatever's left of hope and sanity
and pick the broken bones to bare despair.

Does anybody care?

The question hangs in the fetid air.
I see him stooping there, bleeding hands
searching patiently through the wreckage—
the Scavenger of Souls.
My heart is full of tears;

love and faith fight selfish fears.
What use am I?
He turns and bids me bring my bit of salvage to him—
one treasured soul, a lost and lonely girl.

'Jesus is able to save completely those who come
to God through him…'

LINNET HINTON

IRENE

Barbara Cameron explains: 'Irene was killed by the Peruvian terrorist group Sendero Luminosa, on 21 May 1991. The reason given was her involvement with the distribution of food to the poorer people. The one who shot her was said to be a 16-year-old girl. The funeral was a deeply moving experience.'

I use this prayer when I pray for Christians working in difficult, seemingly impossible circumstances because they have responded to the call of God to go, to love, to incarnate his love.

Irene's been shot. Dead? Jesus…
Her crime? Giving food to the hungry.
I was hungry and you gave me to eat.
Life, how cheap, how fragile.
Victim of the abuse of power,
powerless.

What message for life, this death?
What new call to be heard?

In the midst of violence
a presence of peace.
In the face of death
promoters of life.
In community unity

challenging disunity.
Reflecting on life, grateful,
receptive,
listening, accompanying, incarnating.
Living justly,
loving tenderly,
walking humbly with our God, with his
people.

Contemplative missionaries.

BARBARA CAMERON

POWERLESSNESS

Barbara Cameron reflects on her first two years in Peru. It is a prayer/reflection that many of those who work overseas could echo and a prayer that those working at home could adapt and pray on their behalf. Working with the powerless brings its own rewards, as the following reflections reveal.

Powerless in the face of sickness,
of painful, unnecessary, expensive sickness
of baby, of child, of mother, of youth,
undermining the quality of life, causing premature death.

Powerless in the face of poverty,
of degrading, dehumanizing poverty
that makes beggars of the young, the old,
the handicapped, the sick.

Powerless in the face of strikes,
of recurring, indefinite, crippling strikes
affecting the sick, the poor,
cutting links with family and friends.

Powerless in the face of transport,
of unreliable, insufficient, overcrowded transport
that may or may not run at the scheduled time,
that may or may not follow the scheduled route.

Powerless in the face of bureaucracy,
of red tape, form-filling, power-happy bureaucracy
demanding so much of your time and energy
and patience and money.

Powerless in the face of language,
of fast-flowing, softly spoken, poorly enunciated
language, resulting in not-knowing, misunderstanding
or isolation, in difficulties in communicating.

It is the experience of the 'little people'
in the world of today,
those without health or money or education
or work or status or mobility,
those who haven't a voice,
victims of systems, of history, of politics,
of the abuse of power.

Christ knew powerlessness
in his birth, in his death.

May my experience of powerlessness
lead me to a more real solidarity
with the 'little ones' of this world,
to a deeper compassion,
to a liberating humility
that will open me to receive
from those whose lives touch mine,
that will enrich the quality of my presence
to those who come into my life.

BARBARA CAMERON

IRENE, 23

* 'Hermanita' you called me
and I did feel small
in so many ways.
Small and helpless
in the face of your helplessness,
with your legs that refused to move,
your sores that wouldn't heal.

Small and powerless
in the hospital system,
with insufficient funds, technology and staffing
to improve the quality of your young life.

Small and in awe
of your ability to joke and laugh,
to rise above the frustration
in spite of the pain.

Small and humbled
by the trust you placed in me,
the confidences you shared,
the tears you shed.

Thank you for inviting me into your life, Irene,
as your 'Hermanita'.

BARBARA CAMERON
* HERMANITA MEANS 'LITTLE SISTER'.

ROSARIO, 14

Always there in your wordless world,
abandoned… condemned
to spend your years
in a hospital bed,
dependent on whoever came by
to meet your needs.

So little—so much
to give
by way of your smile.

Somehow your smile communicated
what we all need to hear—
acceptance, welcome,
a reason to hope
when there's no reason to hope.
* Gracias,
Rosario

BARBARA CAMERON
* GRACIAS MEANS 'THANKS'.

NO BEAUTIFUL THOUGHTS

Sometimes the person in need is one's self. We might then need
to pray a prayer asking for help.

No 'beautiful thoughts' today, Lord,
just an overwhelming sense
of failure in this situation,
of helplessness,
of inadequacy,
a sense of being totally unable
to handle it
alone.
Come in, Lord Jesus, and make something
of this miserable heap.

SUE ASHDOWN

✜

Serving in all seasons

The sea ebbs and flows. The moon waxes and wanes. The sun rises and sets. The seasons come and go, drawing us into nature's rhythm of life. The Church, too, woos us into its own rhythm. Advent moves into Christmas. Christmas is followed by Lent. Lent resolves into the crescendo of Easter. After Easter comes the Ascension, followed by Pentecost, and so on.

For the person of prayer, each of these seasons of the spirit presents a particular challenge. Advent, that season of watching and waiting, begs us to reaffirm the Lordship of the Christ who came, the Christ who still comes, the Christ who will come again.

Christmas, the season when we celebrate Christ's first coming, presents us with such a medley of models of self-sacrifice that thoughtful, prayerful Christians find themselves full of desire to emulate the example of Mary and Joseph, the shepherds and the magi, Simeon and Anna. Christmas and Epiphany turn into a time of rededication which, in itself, is a preparation for Lent.

The six-week run-up to Easter that we call Lent can become the springtime of the soul for those who observe it under the guidance of God. Although the soul may have seemed as gnarled and dead as the bare branches of fruit trees in winter, by Holy Week the fruit of the Spirit may have begun to bud again. Watching with Christ in Gethsemane, staying with him as he hangs on the cross, entering into the emptiness of Holy Saturday and marvelling at the mystery of his resurrection can be to the soul what warm sunshine is to tight-shut buds—part of the nurture they need to burst into blossom before maturing into full fruitfulness.

The prayers in this section revel in the Church's seasons and show how, for some people, special days have become landmarks of commitment on the pilgrimage of faith.

ADVENT (NO 1)

Still at last, dear Lord,
   I come to you,
weary from the busyness of a thousand things
   that demand my attention
but longing to feel your touch afresh
   this Christmas-time.
Kindle in me
a love that finds time for you,
that responds to you,
that yearns for your return.
Cause my heart to leap for joy
as I anticipate that great fact of the future—
   your re-entry to earth.
Pour into me the certainty that believes
   that all life is to be lived under the shadow
     of that miraculous return,
the courage to live life your way,
and the resilience to hold on to that hope
   when times are hard
     or the body tired.
Bring me to Christmas Day
   not irritated with Christmas commercialized
but rather rejoicing in the message of the angels:
   to *me*
     this day
       is born
         my Saviour.

IJH

106

ADVENT (NO 2)

O Lord,
my years grow long
and my time short.
Let me make haste with my repentance
and bow both my head and heart.
Let me not stay one day from amendment
lest I stay too long.
Let me cease without delay
to love my own mischief
and to abandon, without a backward look,
the unfruitful works of darkness.
Lord, grant me new watchfulness
to lay hold upon opportunity for good.
Make me at last put on the whole armour of light.
Rank me among them who work for their Lord,
loins girded, lamps burning
till the night shall pass
and the true light shine.
Let me sing the new song,
following the Lamb whithersoever he goes,
loving wheresoever he loves,
doing whatsoever he biddeth
until the perfect day,
the day of the true Advent
when the light comes into the world
for ever and ever.

ERIC MILNER-WHITE [1]

ADVENT (NO 3)

God, keep me steadfast in faith,
   make me joyful in hope
      and untiring in love.
        Now
        and always.
          Amen.

LJH[2]

CHRIST'S SECOND COMING

Lord Jesus Christ,
sometimes, I close my eyes and try to imagine
   what it will be like
when you come again—in glory.
Will the sky blush, as with the sunrise?
Or will it glow as at sunset?
Perhaps your glory will pierce through the clouds
   in a sudden blaze of light?
Who can tell?
And who can tell how that grand reunion
   with loved ones
     will take place?
Amid all these imponderables,
   I cherish the certainty
that when you come to take us home
our loved ones who loved you while they were on earth
   will be with you.
We shall also be with you
in that place where death has lost its sting,
where goodbyes cease,
where there is no more parting
   from those we love
     or from you.

LJH

HE'S COMING BACK

Sometimes, Lord,
it seems too good to be true
that you really are coming back
to take us to be with yourself.
At other times, I confess,
life here on earth seems so good
that I don't want you to come back—
at least, not yet.
Forgive my coldness.
Forgive my doubting.
Fill me afresh with awe
   this Advent
as I anticipate your return
   and heed your command
      to wait in readiness.
Give me the grace
   to change my attitude
   and my lifestyle
so that your coming,
   whenever you come,
      may find me
         greeting you with joy,
            heartfelt thanksgiving,
and an eagerness
   to drop everything instantly
      to be with you
         for ever.

LJH

PREPARING FOR CHRISTMAS

Such a flurry of excitement
   seemed to fill the air
      in town today, Lord.
Women hurried through the bazaar
   clutching poinsettias
      and Christmas cakes
         as well as tinsel to hang on Christmas trees.
Men puffed and panted and heaved and sighed
   as they persuaded huge evergreens
      into their pre-Christmas showplaces—
         outside offices and shops and public buildings.
Father Christmas appeared, too,
   as though from nowhere,
      still clutching his customary dove,
         still gazing at the fairy lights that straddle the streets
          and twinkle above the shoppers.
I became a part of the euphoria, Lord.
I also clutched my poinsettia
   and tinsel,
      pine cones sprayed with silver,
        red candles
        and scarlet ribbons.
'But what are they celebrating?' I wonder.
What makes me rejoice?
You came.
You continue to come.
You will come again.
That's it in a nutshell.
That's the cause of *my* celebration.
As one small boy put it:
'Dear God,
Most people like Christmas because of the presents.
I like Christmas because it's your birthday.'

LJH

110

CHRIST'S BIRTHDAY

As we await your birthday, dear Lord,
grant us a glimpse of the mystery
   of the incarnation.
Cause us to wonder that you,
   the Creator of the universe,
peeled off the splendour and glory
   of the heavenly places
and put on the form of a foetus
   in a woman's womb.
Restore to us
   the ability to stop,
   to ponder,
   to marvel,
   at *you*—
   the radiance of God's glory,
   the flawless expression of the divine nature,
   at God made man,
   God in human form,
   God asking to be touched
     and handled,
     seen,
     known,
     loved.
Teach us to love you without inhibition
that this Christmas
the glow in our hearts
may bring joy to you
and warm the lives
of those less fortunate than ourselves.

LJH

111

NOTHING IMPOSSIBLE WITH GOD

The miracle you did for Zechariah and Elizabeth, O God,
boosts my ability to believe in you,
reminds me that the age of miracles is still not past
and prompts me to marvel at the way
    you intervene in people's lives today.
This Christmas, miracle-working God,
    remove from my eyes the scales of unbelief,
    take from me the heart of stone that refuses to yield to you,
    prepare me so that I am ready to receive you
        with awe and wonder,
        joy and thanksgiving,
        and grateful love
        that flows through me to others.

LJH

LIKE MARY

This prayer was born while I was contemplating the arrival of the
magi on one occasion. As I prayed, I sensed that as the visitors
from the east entered the humble home where the Holy Family
were living, Mary immediately drew their attention away from
herself and on to her child. 'Don't look at me—look at him,' she
seemed to say.

Father,
be with me as I seek to find the right balance
between going out and coming in.
And may my motto always be,
'Don't look at me, look at Jesus.'

LJH

GAZING ON GOD

Mary gazed on God,
   held God,
      gave God to the world.
         Hallelujah.

How can I, Beloved,
   cherish you,
      gaze on you,
         give you to the world?

Yes.
You've told us how:
by cherishing the poor and the sick,
the hungry and those in prison,
the lost and lonely,
we are cherishing you.
As I ponder these mysteries
and thus gaze on you,
give me the grace
to take you into the world—
to my neighbours,
my friends,
and, in particular,
   to those who have never heard
   as well as those working in the world's toughest places.

LJH

LIKE THE SHEPHERDS

This Christmas, dear Lord,
like the shepherds,
I would bow in awed wonder
before the majesty of heaven
revealed in the form of a baby.
Fill me afresh with love
   as I contemplate the mystery.
Reveal yourself to me so that
   like the shepherds
   and the angels
   my heart may be filled with joy.
And transform me so that
   I may become more and more like
   this Christ-child I worship:
   ready to do your will
   in everything
   even at cost to myself.

LJH

A SAVIOUR

To *you* is born a Saviour.

Holy child,
as I take you into my arms,
hold you,
gaze on you,
love and adore you,
the realization dawns afresh that
contemplating you
and serving you
is the antidote to temptation.

I realize, too, that the reason why you came
was to deal with the wayward streak in me
that would so quickly serve self.

To me this day is born my Saviour.
This is mystery.
This is Love—
unearned, undeserved, Love.

My heart desires to return to this loved place often—
to hold and be held,
to cherish and be cherished,
to serve and be served,
to love and be loved,
that I may carry the fruit of this loving
to those who do not know that to them
a Saviour has been born.

LJH

HOLY CHILD

Holy child,
when I turn to you
and hold you,
all other loves pale into insignificance.
For this
I give you humble thanks.

Holy Father,
you have given us this child
to deal with our waywardness.
For this we give you
humble, heartfelt praise.

Holy Spirit,
so work in the hidden parts of me
that my whole being may be turned to the worship and service
of the Beloved
who deigns to be seen
   and heard
      and touched
         and held
            by all who love him.

IJH

CHILD OF MY LOVE

The reason why I came into the world was because
I saw the human predicament—
your predicament.

I loved you.
So I gave my body for you.
It was my pleasure to do this for you,
dear child of my love—
a privilege entrusted to me
by my Father.

Now it rejoices my heart when I see you
receiving me,
relishing my life-giving sacrifice,
savouring my love.

Come often,
for although the threads of the web
in which you are held
have been broken,
you are not yet completely free.

My life and my death,
my body and my blood
can set you free
increasingly.

So come,
child of my love.

A mother pines for her child
when the child seems far away from her.
That is but a pale reflection
of the emptiness I feel
when you seem far away from me.
So come often,
assured that my welcome awaits you.
Let no other loves lure you
up life's cul-de-sacs.
Only stay on the path I show you.
When its going is rough,
be assured that I will be with you
even when you do not feel my presence by your side.

Child of my love,
I am yours
and you are mine
for ever.
LJH

PRAYERS FOR THE NEW YEAR

Jesus, the name high over all
in earth and heaven and sky.
Angels and men before him fall
and devils fear and fly.

Jesus, the name that charms our fears,
that bids our sorrows cease,
'tis music in the sinner's ears
and life and health and peace.

Oh! That the world might taste and see
the triumphs of his grace;
the arms of love that compass me
would all mankind embrace.

Happy if with my latest breath
I might but gasp his name,
preach him to all and cry in death,
'Behold the Lamb.'

CHARLES WESLEY (1707–88)

I said to the man who stood at the gate of the year,
'Give me a light that I may tread safely into the unknown.'
And he replied, 'Go into the darkness and put your hand
    into the hand of God.
That shall be to you better than light and safer than
    a known way!'

MINNIE LOUISE HASKINS, 1908

THE NAMING OF JESUS

'On the eighth day, when it was time to circumcise him, he was named Jesus, the name the angel had given him before he had been conceived' (Luke 2:21). While meditating on Jesus' circumcision and naming on one occasion, I wrote the following prayer.

Lord Jesus, as I embark on yet another year
and with this reminder
   of your supreme sacrifice
rising before my eyes,
I give you myself afresh.
Take me as I am,
take me where you will,
do with me what you will,
this New Year
and always.

LJH

As this New Year unfolds, O God,
enlarge my vision of yourself,
deepen my trust in your love,
increase my faith in the perfection of your purposes,
that when you speak
I may listen,
and when you direct
I may obey—
confident that you will never
   cause your child
      a needless tear.

LJH

LIKE ANNA

Lord Jesus, I would worship you as Anna did,
in spirit and in truth.
Like her I would
submit all my nature to you,
that my conscience may be quickened by your holiness,
my mind nourished by your truth,
my imagination purified by your beauty,
my will surrendered to your purpose,
my heart opened to your love.
Like Anna,
may I turn myself to you
in selfless adoration and ceaseless love and praise.

LJH [3]

EPIPHANY

You prompted the magi
    to abandon their plans, Lord,
to return to their homes
    via a different route.
We, too, have known that prompting
    as you implanted in us
        the desire to abandon our well-laid plans
            for yours.
Beckon us afresh and,
    though we may see no reassuring,
        guiding star,
make unmistakably plain
    the path you would have us tread.

LJH

I sat watching the candles
   burning beside the stable
      this evening, dear Lord.
One, in particular, drew me to itself.
Its flame was so bright,
   so steady,
      so entrancing.
'I want to be like that for you,'
I whispered.
Through Isaiah, you seemed to promise:

'I will make you a light to the nations.'
Thank you.

LJH

LIKE SIMEON

This prayer was inspired while meditating on Simeon's stillness
and effectiveness. The Gospels make only one mention of him
and, as far as we know, he met Jesus only once. Yet his name goes
down in history as one who worshipped Jesus with his whole life
as well as his lips.

I long to be like Simeon, Lord.
So still before you
   that I can hear
      and respond to
         every prompting of your Spirit.
So in tune with you
   that I may become
      a sensitive, loving mouthpiece
         for you.

I yearn, too, to become like Mary:
   ready to have her heart pierced through
      as by a sword.
At the same time, I feel more than a little scared,
   recognizing that there will be times when
      I will rescind this prayer.
So graciously grant me your grace
   to remain open to you
      and to others.

As this new year unfolds,
   grant me the quiet trust
      that watches
         and waits,
            that listens
               and believes
in you
   at all times
      and in all places.

IJH

LIGHT OF THE WORLD

Light of the world,
you shine into my darkness,
where you have become
   my Rescuer,
      my Saviour.

Shine your inextinguishable light
   into every nook and cranny
      of my life
and may that light beam through me
      to others.

IJH

Make me
a still place of light,
a still place of love
of you,
your light radiating,
your love vibrating,
your touch and your healing
far flung and near
to the myriads caught
in darkness, in sickness,
in lostness, in fear.

Make a heart-centre here,
Light of the world.

FROM A PRAYER CARD PRODUCED BY WEST MALLING ABBEY, KENT

PRAYERS FOR PALM SUNDAY

These two prayers were inspired by meditating on the role the
donkey played on the first Palm Sunday. In my meditation, I
'became' the donkey and found it a profoundly moving experience.

Holy Spirit,
create in me more and more
the desire to decrease—
giving space for Jesus to increase.
Give me the strength to plod on:
through crowds,
    through criticism,
        and through crises—
so that Jesus may be proclaimed and known
through who I am
as well as what I say and do.

LJH

Eternal King,
reign in me,
in every part of me.

Use me as you used that donkey:
    to carry you and your message
        wherever you choose to send me:
            to teach,
            to preach,
                to love,
                to serve,
                    to cleanse
                    and to heal. Amen.

LJH

RIDE ON, RIDE ON IN MAJESTY!

Ride on, ride on in majesty!
Hark, all the tribes 'Hosanna' cry;
O Saviour meek, pursue thy road
with palms and scattered garments strowed.

Ride on, ride on in majesty!
In lowly pomp ride on to die;
O Christ, thy triumphs now begin
o'er captive death and conquered sin.

Ride on, ride on in majesty!
The angel armies of the sky
look down with sad and wondering eyes
to see the approaching sacrifice.

Ride on, ride on in majesty!
The last and fiercest strife is nigh;
the Father on his sapphire throne
awaits his own anointed Son.

Ride on, ride on in majesty!
In lowly pomp ride on to die;
bow thy meek head to mortal pain,
then take, O God, thy power, and reign.

HENRY HART MILMAN (1791–1868)

HOLY WEEK

At the beginning of this Holy Week, dear Lord,
I would reaffirm your Lordship
    over my life.
Take the reins and lead me
    where you will.
Take everything I have
    and everything I am.
        Do with me what you will.
May my life glorify your name,
    now and always.

LJH

Oh, make me understand it,
help me to take it in,
what it meant to thee, the Holy One,
to bear away my sin.

KATHERINE A.M. KELLY (1869–1942)

FOR ME (I)

St Ignatius used to encourage his retreatants to meditate on the fact that Jesus' suffering and death was 'for me'. I attempt to do that regularly, which is why several of the prayers in this section contain the recurring phrase, 'For me'. This first prayer was written while I was meditating on Jesus' trial before the Sanhedrin.

Silent, suffering Saviour,
I stand at the brazier,
warm myself by its glow,
see you across the crowded courtyard,
and feel helpless—
powerless.
With my eyes,
with my face,
I communicate the love I feel,
the support I long to give.
But you have gone beyond the place
where any mortal can help you now—
and you are there,
in that condemned place,
because you love me.
You are suffering like this
for me.

IJH

JESUS BEFORE PILATE

A prayer written while meditating on a question Pilate put to Jesus:
'Are you a king?'

Creator of the world,
shine the torchlight of your truth
into the nooks and crannies of my life.
Reveal any inconsistencies and hypocrisies in me
that you would eradicate.
Bring every part of my life into alignment with yourself,
for you are my King.
My longing is that you should reign over me
for ever and ever—
for your glory,
for my wholeness
and for the extension of your kingdom.

IJH

THE FLOGGING

Flogged,
thorn-crowned,
mocked,
spat upon
for me.

Battered,
bruised,
despised,
disabled
for me.

Beloved,
you have given so much for me.
Give me the grace to go on and on
pouring out my lifeblood for you,
counting the cost
but continuing to give and give
like you.

LJH

BEFORE THE CROSS (I)

Written as a result of contemplating the soldiers hammering the
nails into Jesus' hands and feet.

'You can't do it'! I cry.
Yet they hammer the nails into his sacred hands.
They do it *for me*.

I weep.

Lying prostrate on the floor,
my body forming the shape of a cross,
I hear his cry:
  'Father, forgive…'
I give him my life.
I give him my love.
Total surrender.

LJH

FOR ME (2)

This prayer was written as a result of meditating Genesis 3, the story of the Fall. While I was reading this passage, I became acutely aware that Jesus died for me. As I recorded in my prayer journal at the time: 'At the end of that meditation, it was as though a fire burned inside me. I longed to discover how I could help in God's rescue operation of a sinsick world.' Hence, the use of Frances Ridley Havergal's words from the hymn 'Take my life…'

Father,

I am almost lost for words.
That you should sacrifice your Son for me
fills me again with deep, deep gratitude.
Awed.
Speechless.
Sobered.
Surrendered.

How can I withhold anything from you?

I've felt the effects of the medicine of your salvation:
how deeply healing it is
this side of eternity,
let alone the next.

In the light of such love, my Lord,
there are no words.
Only one offering is adequate—
the offering of myself.
So: 'Take my life and let it be
consecrated, Lord, to thee.
Take my moments and my days,
let them flow in ceaseless praise.'

LJH

LET MY HEART CRACK

O Lord, Holy Father, show us what kind of man it is who is hanging for our sakes on the cross, whose suffering causes the rocks themselves to crack and crumble with compassion, whose death brings the dead back to life.

Let my heart crack and crumble at the sight of him. Let my soul break apart with compassion for his suffering. Let it be shattered with grief at my sins for which he dies. And finally let it be softened with devoted love for him. Amen.

ST BONAVENTURE (1221–74)

BEFORE THE CROSS (2)

For drawing me to yourself, I praise you, O God.
For your tender, life-changing love, I worship you.
For the power of your blood to change my sin from scarlet
to snow white, I adore you,
because the only reason for this transformation
is that you loved me enough to die for me.
I feel drops of blood falling
from your beloved wounds
on to my hands, my head, my heart—
intermingling with my blood,
making me clean.
For the wonder of this powerful detergent
I give you humble and heartfelt thanks.

LJH

TREE OF CALVARY

O Tree of Calvary,
send thy roots deep down
into my heart.
Gather together the soil of my heart:
the sands of my fickleness,
the stones of my stubbornness,
the mud of my desires.
Bind them all together.
O Tree of Calvary,
interlace them with thy strong roots,
entwine them with the network
of thy love.

CHANDRAN DEVANESAN [4]

Today he who hung the earth upon the waters
    is hung upon the cross.
He who is King of the angels is arrayed in a crown
    of thorns.
He who wraps the heaven in clouds
    is wrapped in the purple of mockery.
He who in Jordan set Adam free receives blows
    upon his face.
The Bridegroom of the Church is transfixed with nails.
The Son of the Virgin is pierced with a spear.
We worship you, Lord Jesus.
Draw us to yourself with bands of love.
Show us the glory of your resurrection.

LJH [5]

ONLY LOVE

Lord,
I come to you
in the silence of eternity.

I have no words—
only love.
I can hardly bear to look at you
for your love is enormous
and mine is so small.
But the silence is too noisy, Lord,
I hardly dare to breathe—
still the silence,
silence the stillness, Father—
for there is movement yet.

I close my eyes and look at you,
my Father, my Lord, my Love.

You reach out and hold.
I feel the nails
and as your crown of thorns
—my crown of thorns—
pierces your head
—my head—
my eyes weep tears of pain
and my heart bleeds tears of love.

In that tiny, timeless moment of oneness
all my heart can do is to whisper:
    'Father, I am here.'

And across eternity
I hear you whisper back,
    'Child, so am I.'

SUE ASHDOWN

SHEPHERD AND STAR

No one could be crucified in my place.
Even though Simon helped to carry my cross to Calvary,
he was not nailed on it when we reached there.
And my mother could not take my place;
she could only watch my agony and weep for my pain.

But Simon had his place in my sacrifice,
and my mother had her special role of compassion.
And I call men and women in every age
to re-present my passion,
and to act as channels of my life
to those who are searching for me.

It is neither success nor power that will attract them,
but unconditional, self-giving love.
Certainty and spiritual self-confidence
will only make sinners despair;
compassion and self-offering
will build them up and heal them.

I call you to follow my way, the way of the cross,
and when you have allowed my life
to fill you completely,
then I will draw the lost and the hopeless to me
through your hands and your words.

I have appointed you shepherd and star;
the star will give hope to those in darkness,
and guidance to those who are lost,
and the shepherd will feed and protect my people.
    Come, follow me.

RICHARD HOBBS

AUTUMN GLORY

On two occasions, I have celebrated Easter in New Zealand where, of course, Easter time comes in autumn and not spring. On both occasions I have missed the spring images and fumbled to find pictures that are married to autumn. Here, Linnet Hinton, whom I met in New Zealand, has done what I failed to do and I have been helped on many occasions by her prayer of praise.

Liquid amber,
foliage flaming
in sunkist splendour,
glorious extravagance
amid evergreen security,
magnificent
in dying—
at Easter.

Eternal Lord,
you shed your life
like autumn leaves
blood-red falling
from the tree,
lovelit to the end,
a nimbus of glory
against the darkest night,
majestic in your dying—
that Easter.

You are the Vine,
I, a branch,
as you are, I must be.
You blazed the way
to life through death.

I want to follow you,
to drop my finite foliage
too, in radiance
of self-giving love.
Saviour, I pray,
put your glory on display
in my dying—
this Easter, and always.

LINNET HINTON

HALLELUJAH! CHRIST IS RISEN!

Each year, when my husband and I lived in Cyprus, we would lead an Easter retreat. It began with a celebration of the Last Supper on Maundy Thursday evening and ended on Easter Monday. Most of the meetings took place outside—in the olive groves or beside a cave that was reminiscent of the garden tomb. On Easter Sunday morning, while it was still dark, we walked to this 'tomb' and waited in silence for the sun to rise. The silence was occasionally punctuated with music played on a portable cassette player. At sunrise, there on the hillside overlooking the sea, which shimmered in the rays of the sun, we worshipped the risen Lord. The prayer that follows came from a thankful heart on one of those wonderful mornings.

I saw you in the fullness of the moon
    that lighted my path
        on the way to the tomb.
I saw you in the dove-shaped cloud
    that hovered over the hills
        as we waited for sunrise.
I saw you in the sun which
        slid over the mountain
            in all its majesty—
                thrilling us with its appearance.

I saw you in the liquid gold cross
   traced on the sea
      by the rays of the rising sun.

I worshipped you
   in the strains of the aria from Handel's *Messiah*
      that heralded that sunrise:
         'I know that my Redeemer lives...'

I heard and felt you when,
   like the angel,
      I sat outside the garden tomb
      and wanted to shriek:
         'He is not here... he is risen!'

Joy.
Pure joy.
IJH

ON RETREAT

More and more people are discovering the value of quiet days and
retreats where we can step off the treadmill for a few hours, engage
in some spiritual stocktaking and refocus by fixing our gaze on
God. The prayers that follow have been written during such times
of stillness, although this short section starts with a plea from God.

THE ONE VITAL THING

*See communion with myself as your highest activity... there are no
places on earth where this activity is impossible...*

   *Temptations to restrict the activity of communion with me are often
disguised as 'pressing duty', often involve misuse of time which will
contribute nothing to your progress.*

My child, treasure time spent, consciously, with me, as I supply need for the hours ahead. Such communion, far from mere escaping, is dynamic in its essence… and is indispensable for you. You were not meant to live without my resources!

Only one thing is vital… (Luke 10:24).

JOHN WOOLLEY [6]

NOTICING

This was written on a residential retreat.

'Too busy to be here?'
Too busy to be!
To rest and enjoy this:
I in you, you in me.
Too busy to wonder,
wander, just you and me.

My pace becomes slower,
the child starts to show.
What do trees feel like?
How do things grow?
I wander, I wonder,
what truths will he show?

The first day, I see it—
its occupant gone.
The form is near perfect,
but being moves on.
That place that is broken
has birthed a new song.

Cicada's wings—so fragile,
unseen by its eyes;
yet trusting its maker,
it unfolds them, and flies!
Things revealed to the infant
are hid from the wise.

Can *I* trust you, Lord?
Step forth from *my* shell?
Beat heart's wings I can't see?
To go where? I can't tell.
Your love, it allures me,
with words that compel:

'Come to me, learn of me,
I do all things well.'

DAVID CRAWLEY

RENEWAL

I came to you—
    frightened, broken, naked—
    ashamed and lonely!
        You were to me—
        a haven of refuge,
a deep gentle spring
of refeshing hope,
    a gentle rain,
washing away dusty fears,
    a warm summer sun
calling forth *new life*!
        Always—
            a Guiding Light.

ISABEL RADNETT[7]

BURNED OUT

This prayer and the next were first prayed among the pine trees in the Troodos Mountains in Cyprus, where I was meditating on the verse, 'Jesus Christ laid down his life for us. And we ought to lay down our lives for one another' (1 John 3:16).

The burned out pine tree draws me
   as a magnet draws iron filings.
I gaze long and hard at its woundedness:
   at the resin dangling from it,
     at the sun highlighting
      its richness and redness.
I feel the breeze broadcasting the fragrance
   of its perfume.

I marvel that the tree has not only survived:
   it thrives,
     towering in all its splendour
      above the great gash caused
      by a streak of lightning.

'It's possible to be burned out
   yet live,'
     the scene whispers.

A nearby tree now beckons me.
   On its slender trunk
     I see a figure hanging:
      not desolate
       but triumphant.
        The Crucified.

My heart leaps for joy.
I am no longer alone
but one with you.

You give me your perspective.
    You lure me into the gash in the pine tree's side.
        You show me that there
            I can shelter from the wind.

May my wounds, Beloved,
    provide shelter
        for your hurting ones
            today and always.

LJH

LOVE REKINDLED

I'm sitting in the forest
    hurting,
        burdened,
            questioning.
Two great-tits come to visit.
They hop on to the branch of the great pine
    under whose branches
        I'm sheltering from the sun.
        They sit.
            They sing.
                They disappear.

'I know when one such fledgling falls,'
    you whisper.
        'And you are more precious to me
            than the smallest sparrow.'

I marvel.
    You know me through and through,
        yet I matter to you.

I transfer to you afresh
   the burden of my unanswered questions
      and my love for you is rekindled.

Thank you.

LJH

HOMECOMING

This was written while praying with Frank Wesley's famous picture
of the Prodigal Son. In this picture, the Indian artist has painted
the prodigal in such a way that it is clear that, unless the father
holds on to him, he will keel over. I frequently find consolation as
I gaze at the imagery that gave birth to the following prayer.

Father,
as I gazed at that picture of the prodigal
clasped in your arms,
feelings of relief swept over me.
I know it's where I am;
I know it's where I need to be.
I've given so much,
experienced so much.
Now, I just need to rest
in that place of true, undemanding homecoming,
the safety and security
of your tender heart.

No words are needed.
I can collapse,
nestle
and be.

LJH

Father,
may your love so spring up within me
that it overflows from me continually.
Remind me that if the source is clogged up
I have nothing to give.
Of myself I am nothing.

LJH

GUNSHOTS

On the island where I used to live, twice a week in the 'hunting season', men scoured and scarred the beautiful countryside that surrounded my home, hunting for birds to shoot and pickle. As often happened, on one of my quiet days gunshots coincided with the sound of the church bells that called the villagers to worship. The bells reminded us that we were being prayed for by the village priest. Those twin sounds—the shots and the bells—made a profound impact on me. I thought of the birds that would be left half dead, flapping injured wings that had lost their ability to fly. And I thought of villagers who would be consoled by God in the precincts of the church. This prayer seemed to rise from somewhere deep within me:

Keep me, O Lord,
from slaughtering others
with the witch-hunt of my gossip,
    with the gunshots of my tongue,
        with the cruelty of neglect.

Rather, make of my heart
    a holy home where
        people can come,
            find consolation,
                peace
                    and *you*.

LJH

MAGNIFY THE LORD WITH ME

O most high
    and glorious God,
        come speak into my confusion.

In your awe-filled presence,
    silence so often sounds most powerful.
Yet I often feel that if I keep my peace,
    the rocks themselves will cry out.
But if I speak, what should I say?

My love for you prompts me to speak,
    even though it sometimes feels like stammering.
      I love you, Lord.
        I adore you.
          I bow down before you.
I thank you for your generous gifts of grace:
    the awesome glory of the sunrise and the sunset,
    the glory of colours,
    the comfort of the voices of loved ones.
I love you, Lord.
    As I witness your greatness—
    your glory,
    and as I feel your tender loving care,
    grant me the grace to love you more and more,
    to serve you as you deserve to be served,
    to worship you
      with endless wonder
        and ceaseless praise.
This I pray for the glory of Jesus.
LJH[8]

✛

Enjoying God's world

'Creation can become a prime source of dialogue with Jesus as we seek to grow in our love relationship with him...'

All creation bears the traces of God and will lead the spiritually sensitive observer back to the Trinity through Christ...

If we look and listen with the eyes and ears of faith, all creation will 'declare the glory of God' (Psalm 19:1), which is in Jesus Christ, the divine Word of the Trinity...

Whoever is not enlightened by such brilliance of things created
  must be blind;
whoever is not awakened by their mighty voice must be deaf;
whoever fails to praise God for all his works must be dumb;
whoever fails to discover the First Principle through these signs
  must be a fool.

JOHN MICHAEL TALBOT [1]

I believe these truths passionately. I teach them to others and delight to suggest ways in which would-be people of prayer can discover them for themselves. So I sat on a deserted beach one day, fingering the multicoloured miniature stones that lined the shore, basking in the warmth of the setting sun, relishing the song of the sea and expecting God to speak through these signs of his craftsmanship. But God seemed to be strangely silent that day.

Pondering the mystery of the seeming silence, I wandered along 'my' beach, the place where I go most days to pray, and I continued along my hour-long prayer walk. This walk took me off the beach, through orange groves and past vineyards to the brow of a hill that affords a panoramic view of one of the most idyllic parts of the island of Cyprus. As though I was seeing this breathtaking view for the very first time, I stopped to stare at the medley of colours above and below me: the slate blue of the sky merging with the azure blue of the sea, the silver-green of the olive trees mottled with the ambers and golds of the walnut leaves and the browns and bronzes of the vines. As I marvelled at this harmony, I listened to Vespers being chanted by the birds. 'What are you saying to me through the mysteries before me?' I whispered to God. Clear as a bell, three words popped into my mind: 'Just enjoy them.' I laughed. And I obeyed. Consequently, I returned home, no longer tense or intense but rather renewed in body, mind and spirit.

'Just enjoy them.' Those words still influence me. I find them curiously liberating. They helped me to see that God doesn't want us to become over-intense in our relationship with him. He wants us to relax and find joy in his renewing and renewable gifts.

A few days later, I looked on my bookshelves for books about joy. There were volumes on grief and depression, spiritual warfare and marriage problems, loneliness, conflict and the forgiveness of sins—but none on joy. I knew that I had two books on the subject in England but they were not on my shelves in Cyprus. One was *Joy* by Louis Evely.[2] As I explained in my book *Listening to Others*,[3] this Jesuit priest claims that the inability to receive joy is a universal problem; that although Jesus made us depositaries of his joy and although Christianity is a religion of joy, Christians somehow seem to have missed their entry into joy's fullness. We are better disposed to be sorrowful with Christ and to share his sufferings than to become participators in resurrection joy.

I turned to Genesis 1, where we read that, on the sixth day, having created the world, 'God saw all that he had made, and it was very good' (v. 31).

God resting
God relishing
God marvelling
at the mysteries he had made.
God savouring
God enjoying
God embracing
the wonders
his Creator-hands had crafted.

My mind went to the poet Gerard Manley Hopkins. Surely, here is someone who discovered the secret of enjoying, savouring, relishing, marvelling, embracing God's world. Was not that the reason he could write memorable lines like these?[4]

The world is charged with the grandeur of God.
It will flame out, like shining from shook foil...

Nothing is so beautiful as Spring—
    When weeds, in wheels, shoot long and lovely and lush...
    The glassy peartree leaves and blooms, they brush
    The descending blue; that blue is all in a rush
With richness; the racing lambs too have fair their fling.
What is all this juice and all this joy?
    A strain of the earth's sweet being in the beginning
In Eden garden...

Glory be to God for dappled things—
    For skies of couple-colour as a brinded cow;
        For rose-moles all in stipple upon trout that swim...

The prayers in this section start with the plea that we may learn to find God everywhere. They continue with unashamed expressions of enjoyment of the wonders of God's world.

GOD WITHIN, GOD EVERYWHERE

This prayer, written in 1514, is as relevant today as on the day it was penned.

God be in my head,
    and in my understanding;
God be in my eyes,
    and in my looking;
God be in my mouth,
    and in my speaking;
God be in my heart,
    and in my thinking;
God be at my end,
    and at my departing.

FROM THE SARUM PRIMER, 1558

JOY

As the hand is made for holding
and the eye for seeing,
you have fashioned me, O Lord,
for joy.
Share with me the vision
to find that joy everywhere:
in the wild violet's beauty,
in the lark's melody,
in the face of a steadfast man,
in a child's smile,
in a mother's love,
in the purity of Jesus.

LJH[5]

THE BEACH

Great waves, crashing, foaming,
   running up the sand.
To stop gently at its edge.
   Wonder!

M. CHANEL O'DONNELL

I PRAISE YOU

For setting me free
  to delight in
    donkeys and trees,
      sun and moon,
        sky and stars,
          extravagant colours
            and miniature wild flowers
I praise you, O God.

For begging me to enjoy
  the filigree-fragrance of the almond blossom,
    the blues and turquoises of the sea,
      star-like grasses
        and open-faced anemones
I praise you, dear Lord.

For prompting me to chuckle
  at the antics of monkeys
    and ducks
      and turtles
      and fish
I praise you, Creator God.

For the sheer enjoyment of your world
I give you thanks.

LJH

A COUNTRY WALK

I walked today, Lord,
such a glorious walk:
   sparkling air,
      fresh sea breeze,
        clear blue sky,
            uninterrupted sunshine.

'Look at the birds', you insisted.
I did.
They chattered,
   they soared,
      they swooped
        and some paused
           to drink from the puddles
              formed by last night's storm.

'Contemplate the lilies,' you whispered.
I did.
At a carpet of purple, pink and cream anemones.
Oh! And I picked blackberries,
found three big pine cones that begged to decorate our home
   for Christmas,
collected windfalls—juicy mandarin oranges—
then came back to bake bread.
While kneading the dough,
through the kitchen window I spied
   a huge cheese-shaped moon peeping over the mountain range.
'My gift,' you seemed to say,
'to remind you that I love you.'

Joy.
Tears of joy.
True contentment.

LJH

HIS VOICE

His voice, never silent,
rolls along the shore,
surges on to the sands,
echoes off cliffs,
thunders over falls,
roars down mountainsides,
drum-beats drought-taut ground
in continuous communication
with creation.
A vibrant cascade
of life-giving sound.

It sings in my veins,
throbs in my heart,
stirs my stagnant spirit
to a crescendo of desire.

I drink it in deeply
yet thirst for more,
unsatisfied until at last
my calloused ears can hear
beyond fluid sound
the solid shape of words.

'And his voice was like the sound of many waters.'
LINNET HINTON[6]

RAINDROPS

Raindrops dangling
    like bright baubles
        on the fronds of the bottle-brush tree.
Enjoy them.
LJH

SUNRISE

I wrote this on the rooftop of a guest house where my husband and I were staying in Pokhara, Nepal. The owner of the guest house had hammered on our door when light began to dawn to alert us to the fact that if we went up on to the rooftop of the house straight away, we would be rewarded with a stunning sunrise. The rooftop afforded a breathtaking view of Nepal's famed Annapurna range of mountains—Annapurna One, Two and Three and the Fishtail Mountain—once seen, never forgotten.

The marvels of your creation bring me
    endless delight, dear Lord:
  the crescent moon,
  the one, solitary star shining so steadfastly
    from the grey-blue sky,
  the chatter of the birds,
  the majesty of the mountains,
  the glow of the heavens,
  and the shafts of light that signal
      the sun's rising.

The glow is subsiding,
the sky turning the colour of opals.
Clouds enshroud the mountains.
They tell me you are holy
and remind me of your Shekinah glory.
One puffy cloud turns from grey to pink.
Now another,
  now another,
yet the sun is nowhere to be seen
so the mountains remain a solid black mass.

Breathless with wonder
  I wait and watch.
The clouds, now a purply-pink, disperse.

The unseen sun tinges
    first the peak of the Fishtail Mountain,
    now the crest of Annapurna One.
The pink is spreading from the Fishtail's tip
    right down its giant sides
        and Annapurna Three begins to glint in the glory.

Annapurna One is now ablaze
    and birdsong fills the air:
    crows cawing,
    a sparrow chirping,
    the tree-top choir carolling
while Annapurna Two reflects the sun's light.

At last, the sun, a resplendent red ball,
slides slowly and surreptitiously over the treetops,
where it hangs like a silent, majestic balloon—
further transforming the mountaintops
    from starkness to softness,
    from grimness to glory.

The ever-changing panorama before me
banishes yesterday's deep-down weariness,
replacing it with a feeling of refreshment.
Oh! The wonder of responding to your invitation
    to *enjoy* your wonderful world.

LJH

SUNSET (I)

One part of the sky
seemed like a frothing, foaming sea tonight, Lord—
not white suds
but swirls of pink
tinged with purple.

Across the steel blue of a cloudless patch of sky
someone seemed to be stretching streamers—
fluorescent pink that changed before my eyes
from pink to vermilion to purple.
Cars rushed by—
occupants oblivious of the pageant in the sky—
while I stood riveted,
awed,
transfixed by the grandeur.
Was it colour like this that prompted the psalmist to sing:
'The heavens declare the glory of God'?
As now, so then, did you throw open
the casements of heaven and allow him to gaze on
your beauty,
your majesty,
your magnificence,
your splendour?
Who can tell?
For beckoning me from my desk
and thrilling me afresh with this glimpse of your glory,
I give you humble and heartfelt thanks.

LJH

THE CREATOR

Almighty Creator, you who made all things:
the world cannot express all your glories,
even though the grass and the trees should sing.
You have wrought such a multitude of wonders
that they cannot be equalled or expressed.
So it is not hard work to praise you, Holy Trinity,
nor to praise you, Son of Mary.

LJH[7]

154

A SACRIFICE OF PRAISE

For the beauty of the earth,
for the beauty of the skies,
for the love which from our birth
over and around us lies,
Christ our God, to you we raise
this our sacrifice of praise.

For the beauty of each hour
of the day and of the night,
hill and vale, and tree and flower,
sun and moon and stars of light,
Christ our God, to you we raise
this our sacrifice of praise.

For the joy of ear and eye,
for the heart and mind's delight,
for the mystic harmony
linking sense to sound and sight,
Christ our God, to you we raise
this our sacrifice of praise.

For the joy of human love,
brother, sister, parent, child,
friends on earth and friends above,
pleasures pure and undefiled,
Christ our God, to you we raise
this our sacrifice of praise.

For each perfect gift divine
to our race so freely given,
joys bestowed by love's design,
flowers of earth and fruits of heaven,
Christ our God, to you we raise
this our sacrifice of praise.

F.S. PIERPOINT (1835–1917)

SUNSET (2)

This prayer was written at 2.30 one morning. I woke and lay in bed overwhelmed by the love of God. Into his love I lifted those dearest to me, and I felt at peace. The image that flooded my mind was of the setting sun shimmering on the sea near my home. My mind went to Jesus' injunction, 'When you pray, say, "Father…".' I went into my study to write. As I finished writing the prayer, my eyes lighted on a photograph on the wall—of a friend of mine cuddling his baby. The child is nestling his head into his father's neck and the father has his arms wrapped around his son. He is enfolding him in love, gazing at him adoringly. They are, indeed, two yet one.

Father,
as the soon-setting sun
pours its rays on to the shimmering sea,
   warming it,
      transforming it,
so you beam the radiance of your life-giving love
on to me,
   into me,
consoling me,
transforming me.

For the wonder of this undeserved,
      unconditional,
         healing love
I praise you.
I bask in it,
   absorb it,
      relish it,
         abandon myself to it,
            delight in it.

I plumb its depths
    and begin to understand the mystery:
        I am in you
            and you are in me.
We are separate,
        different,
yet gloriously one.

LJH

SAVOURING SOUNDS

The soughing of the wind.
The roaring of the sea.
The rustling of the leaves of the walnut trees.
The carolling of the birds.
The scrunch, scrunch, scrunch of my lone footsteps.
I'm enjoying to the full,
Lord God,
your mysterious gift of hearing.

LJH

THANK YOU

Goats grazing,
    sun setting,
        wagtails paddling,
            wildflowers beckoning,
                birds chattering,
and the first white almond-blossom peeping
    from a tree that looks oh! so dead.

Thank you.

LJH

WAS IT YOU?

Someone smudged the sky with pink
   this morning, Lord.
Was it you?

Someone even painted the sea pink.
Was that you?

No camera could capture
   the mystery,
     the majesty,
      the magic
of those flamingo pink
   smears and smudges and streaks
     mingling with the cloudless blue
      of a winter's sky.
No paintbrush could colour the sea
   salmon pink.
It must have been you.

Someone filled the air
   with birdsong this morning, Lord.
Was it you?
Did you set the cockerels crowing,
   the robins warbling,
     the sparrows twittering,
      the great-tits singing 'pink-pink', 'see-saw'?
No human visionary could dream up the dawn chorus.
It must have been you.

LJH

ENGLAND IN SEPTEMBER

When people have served God overseas for even a short while, one of the problems they face on their return to the homeland is 'reverse culture shock'—the shock of being suddenly confronted with what once was familiar but now appears strange, even alien. In September 1995, I made a brief stopover in England and wondered how I would find it. I wrote the following as a result of travelling through Kent by train—thrilled at the beginning of autumn.

For
sparkling air and
scarlet berries;
contemplative cows
and luscious grass;
oak leaves
and acorns,
silver birch trees
and golden leaves;
friendly train guards
and silent companions;
for this faint familiarity
resurrecting a glut of happy memories,
I give you thanks,
O God.

For the ease of rerooting,
for these simple pleasures,
for the sense of security
and joy of belonging,
I praise you from the very depths
of my being.

LJH

RIOTOUS COLOUR

The russets of the vineyards,
the scarlets of the poinsettias,
the purples of the bougainvilleas,
the pinks of the geraniums;
thank you, God, for riotous colour.

The soft-silver of the olive trees,
the muted mauve of the grape hyacinths,
the speedwell-blue of the sky,
soil the colour of coffee;
thank you, God, for quiet colours.

The greens and lemons of the variegated ivies,
the yellows and browns of the bronzing pomegranate trees,
the purples and pinks of a speckled sky at sunset,
the rainbow of colours created by corals;
thank you, God, for mottled colours.

The wispy-whiteness of the clouds,
the sapphire-blueness of the sea,
the virgin greenness of the meadows,
the sleek-brownness of the sheep.

Thank you, God, for creating colours—
    colours that dazzle,
        colours that soothe,
            colours that move,
                colours that harmonize,
                    colours that fill endless hours
                        with sheer delight.

IJH

SIMPLE PLEASURES

I picked blackberries today, Lord.
Not plump, juicy ones like I'd pick in England,
but blackberries just the same—
enough to stew with apples for supper.
I collected mandarin oranges, too—
windfalls lying beneath trees
laden with fruit that looks so much like
   lights adorning the branches.
Oh! And I saw a robin—
red-breasted,
open-beaked,
singing full throttle
in the corner of the garden
it frequented last year.
Such simple pleasures.
Were these the mysteries
you surveyed
on that first sabbath day
when you stopped and stared and confessed:
'It's good'?

LJH

GLORY

Leaden sky,
   steel-grey sea
      a great-tit
      swinging on the bottle-brush tree
and your sign of promise, Lord,
   arching right across the valley:
      a double rainbow.
      Glory!

LJH

THE BEAUTY OF GOD

Ah, Lord God,
if the things you have made are so wonderful,
how exceedingly beautiful and ravishing
you must be in yourself.

LJH⁸

O Lord, our Lord,
how majestic is your name in all the earth!
You have set your glory
   above the heavens…
When I consider your heavens,
   the work of your fingers,
the moon and the stars,
   which you have set in place,
[I ask] what is man that you are
   mindful of him?

PSALM 8:1, 3–4a

* AOTEAROA—MY HOMELAND

Aotearoa—
   my homeland so beautiful,
      freshness and greenness
         restoring to wholeness.

Rock pools and seascapes
   shimmering,
      glimmering,
         sunlight a-filtering.

Sky and sea oneness
   stretching beyond us,
      infinity breathless.

Seagulls a-crying,
　　dipping and diving,
　　　　curving and gliding
　　　　　　in graceful air-riding...

Bush walks abundant,
　　ferns, mosses and creepers,
　　　　silence and stillness,
　　　　　　peace deep within us.

Waterfall, cascades, streams
　　babbling in chorus—
breakers, foam surges,
　　white fountains enormous.

Bird songs resounding,
　　trilling and thrilling,
　　　　heartstirring, joyous,
　　　　　　spellbinding, rapturous.

I look at the sun as its rays pierce my being,
　　up, upwards it draws me,
　　　　it beckons so strongly,
　　　　　　up, upwards in spirit
　　　　　　　　to the warmth and true brightness.

Sun, Sonship within me
　　embracing, dissolving,
　　　　dancing in oneness
　　　　　　to tunes ever timeless.

O praise to you, Son, Creator, and Spirit,
　　breathing forth beauty in all things around us,
　　　　renewing, restoring, enhancing, creating,
I praise you and thank you for my homeland so bounteous.

MOIRA ROSS (* AOTEAROA IS THE MAORI NAME FOR NEW ZEALAND)

163

GODSONG

I heard your melody in water, air and earth,
sung gently in clear flowing stream
and whispered on the summer breeze,
with the swelling largo of the sweet-smelling
earth as it nurtures spring growth
and mellows autumn fruitfulness.
In the call of the tui and the bellbird,
in the shrilling of the seagulls whirling over
beach and bach*
and in the lamb's bleating cry for its mother's milk,
in the counterpoint of sun and shadow,
of calm and storm,
I recognized the myriad patterns
of your song in all creation
and heard it all as Godsong.

I listened to humansong pulsing with life's melody,
composed with love, enriched by compassion,
harmonized in forgiveness, sparkling with laughter,
renewed in work and play,
in friendship and cooperation,
and all this I heard
as Godsong.

I sang your melodies, I joined in your harmonies,
faltering at times, but learning more confidently
to participate in Godsong
until at some point I found myself out of rhythm,
out of time, my life sounding discordant,
off beat, off pitch.
Where now is Godsong,
where now is humansong,
where now is my song
among the jangling sounds

and disjointed rhythms
of disappointment,
anger, frustration,
intolerance, irritation,
failure, and isolation?

What happened to the
beautiful melodies,
the mature harmony,
the contrapuntal movement,
the swelling crescendos
and gently fading rallentandos?
Where are the runs and trills
that made my song
humansong?

Tune my heart, friend Jesus, to learn anew your music.
Sing for me your true humansong,
that I may sing my song in harmony with you,
and hear again in my life
Godsong.

I heard your whistle in the summer,
when loving friendship
flourished on the sands of time
and your song was as a sweet,
clear cantor's note calling forth
a singing heart within me,
gathering in confidence
and swelling with joy,
so that once more my song merged
with your song,
not always in perfect harmony,
sometimes still faltering,
but truly humansong.

Once more I hear
your song in wind and rain,
in sun and sea and surf,
in the rhythms of birth and death,
in family and friends;
sometimes in the full swelling harmony
of broad daylight,
sometimes faintly on the night air
comes the music of life
that I recognize again
as Godsong.

JOAN PARKER (* 'BACH' IS THE KIWI WORD FOR A HOLIDAY HOME)

DREAMING

How sweet
to sit
alone
and dream
in peace,
of this
and that.
Of trees,
the rain,
bright light,
cool streams,
the wind,
birds' songs,
the sun.
To see
in mind
the waves
that curl
and break

on sands,
near cliffs.
To speak
to God
of joy
and love,
of life,
his Son,
our hopes.
To watch
a maid
beside
her babe
asleep
upon
the hay.

To think
and dwell
on joys
we've had
and friends
we loved
so well.
To close
the door
and still
the noise
and be
alone
with God.

M. MARCELLA ROACHE

167

NATURE PRAYER

You paint the sunrises and sunsets.
You are the songwriter and conductor of the birds.
You are the one who sends the water for the clouds,
    rivers and earth.
You shape the mountains and arrange the stars
    in the sky.
You are the lifegiver and midwife
    for the animals of the fields.
You shape me and mould me and I thank you.
Never let me forget or neglect you.
Let me always respond to your thirst
    for my love.
And even when I feel worthless…
You be the power of love,
    the force of your Spirit within
    —loving you as you deserve to be loved
    —thanking you and praising you.

'CATHY'

THE COBWEB

I slept; yet in the dewy night
the spider spun on—
weaving a thread of silver
into a web so fine.

Sometimes patching up
where the wind had come to tease.
Welcoming the dewdrops
to hang as silver beads.
    Wonder!

CHANEL O'DONNELL

NOTES

Introduction

1 T. Hudson, *Christ-following*, Hodder and Stoughton, 1996, p. 97
2 St Mary Euphrasia, *Embrace the World*, Sisters of the Good Shepherd, Province of York, 1993, p. 69
3 Ibid., p. 69
4 Ibid., p. 45
5 Ibid., p. 76
6 Ibid., p. 76

Enjoying intimacy with God

1 *Love: A Guide for Prayer*, St Mary's Press, 1985, p. 11
2 Adaptation of a prayer by Isaac of Stella (1100–69)
3 *I Am With You*, O Books, 2005, p. 10
4 Adaptation of the First Prayer from the Liturgy of St John Chrysostom
5 Adaptation of a prayer by St Symeon the New Theologian
6 *I Am With You*, p. 10
7 *The Oxford Book of Prayer,* OUP, 2002, pp. 56–57
8 Adaptation of a prayer by Dean Eric Milner-White, *My God, My Glory*, SPCK, 1994
9 *Embrace the World*, p. 69
10 Quoted by John Veltri SJ in *Orientations Vol 1: a collection of helps for prayer*, Loyola House, 1979, p. 46
11 Adaptation of Ephesians 3:14–21

Help me to say 'Yes'

1 Henri Nouwen, *Life of the Beloved: Spiritual Living in a Secular World*, Crossroad, 2002
2 *Heal My Heart, O Lord*, Eagle, 1997, p. 38
3 *RNDM Poetry*
4 *Set Me Free*, Spectrum Publications, 1972
5 See www.grailsociety.org.uk
6 'My Peruvian Journey', *RNDM Poetry*
7 Adaptation of a prayer by Cardinal Newman
8 *I Am With You*, p. 18
9 *A Silence and a Shouting*, The Leprosy Mission, 1982
10 *Embrace the World*, p. 8

When times are tough

1 Louis Evely, *In the Christian Spirit*, Search Press, Ltd, 1969
2 Charles Elliott, *Praying the Kingdom: Towards a Political Spirituality*, Paulist Press, 1986
3 *I Am With You*
4 Ibid., p. 5
5 Ibid., p. 26
6 Ibid., p. 1
7 From *Heal My Heart, O Lord*

Going where it hurts

1 J. Neville Ward, *Five for Sorrow, Ten for Joy: a Consideration of the Rosary*, Cowley Publications, 1985
2 *Keep Me Singing: Songs of Pilgrimage*, Bible College of Victoria
3 Ibid.
4 Adaptation of a prayer by St Anselm

Serving in all seasons

1 Last three lines from *My God, My Glory*.
2 Adaptation of a blessing for the first Sunday of Advent, from *The Sunday Missal*, Collins, 1997
3 Adaptation of a prayer by George Appleton
4 From *The Cross is Lifted*, Friendship Press, 1954, p. 58
5 Adaptation of 'Hymns of Good Friday' from *The Lenten Triodion*
6 *I Am With You*, p. 21
7 *RNDM Poetry*, Canada
8 Inspired by a prayer of Richard Foster

Enjoying God's world

1 *The Lover and the Beloved: Face to Face with Christ in Prayer*, Marshall Pickering, 1987
2 Louis Evely, *Joy*, Burns & Oates, 1968
3 Joyce Huggett, *Listening to Others*, Hodder & Stoughton, 2005
4 'God's grandeur', 'Spring' and 'Pied beauty' from Gerard Manley Hopkins, *Poems and Prose*, Penguin, 1970
5 Adaptation of a Celtic prayer
6 *Keep Me Singing*, p. 33
7 Adaptation of an early Welsh poem
8 Adaptation of a prayer by Henry Suso (1300–66)

INDEX OF FIRST LINES

174